HOT TOPICS

JACK CHICK AND DAVID W. DANIELS

CHICK PUBLICATIONS
ONTARIO, CALIFORNIA

For a complete list of distributors near you,
call (909) 987-0771, or visit **www.chick.com**

Copyright ©2008 Jack T. Chick LLC

Published by:
CHICK PUBLICATIONS
PO Box 3500, Ontario, Calif. 91761-1019 USA
Tel: (909) 987-0771
Fax: (909) 941-8128
Web: www.chick.com
Email: postmaster@chick.com
Printed in the United States of America

ISBN: 978-07589-0721-9

Buy a copy of this book at:
www.chick.com/catalog/books/1270.asp

CONTENTS

Introduction

Over the years, Jack Chick has written many gospel tracts on hot-button issues. Some were so hot it was difficult to hand one to a stranger. They might think you were accusing them of participating in the sin targeted by that tract.

Though many soul winners deemed some tracts "too hot to handle," Jack Chick and David W. Daniels still felt strongly that the messages in these tracts needed to get out since the sins they targeted are rapidly expanding in our culture.

People need to know that God's judgment is hanging over this nation unless we repent of these sins. They also need to know that Christ can redeem them from even these most horrific of evils.

This book includes six of these hot-button tracts, complete and updated, accompanied by in-depth research and a discussion with Jack Chick and David W. Daniels on these little-talked-about subjects. Readers can follow the discussion by noting that JTC is Jack Chick and DWD is David W. Daniels.

Vital information is presented that soul winners need to know as they minister to sinners caught in these perversions and delusions. This book will awaken and provoke Bible believers to better confront these vital subjects in their soul winning.

George Collins, Editor
Chick Publications

Some people believe they have the right to do anything they want with your kids — even if it kills them. Should they have that right? And is there any way to stop them?

7

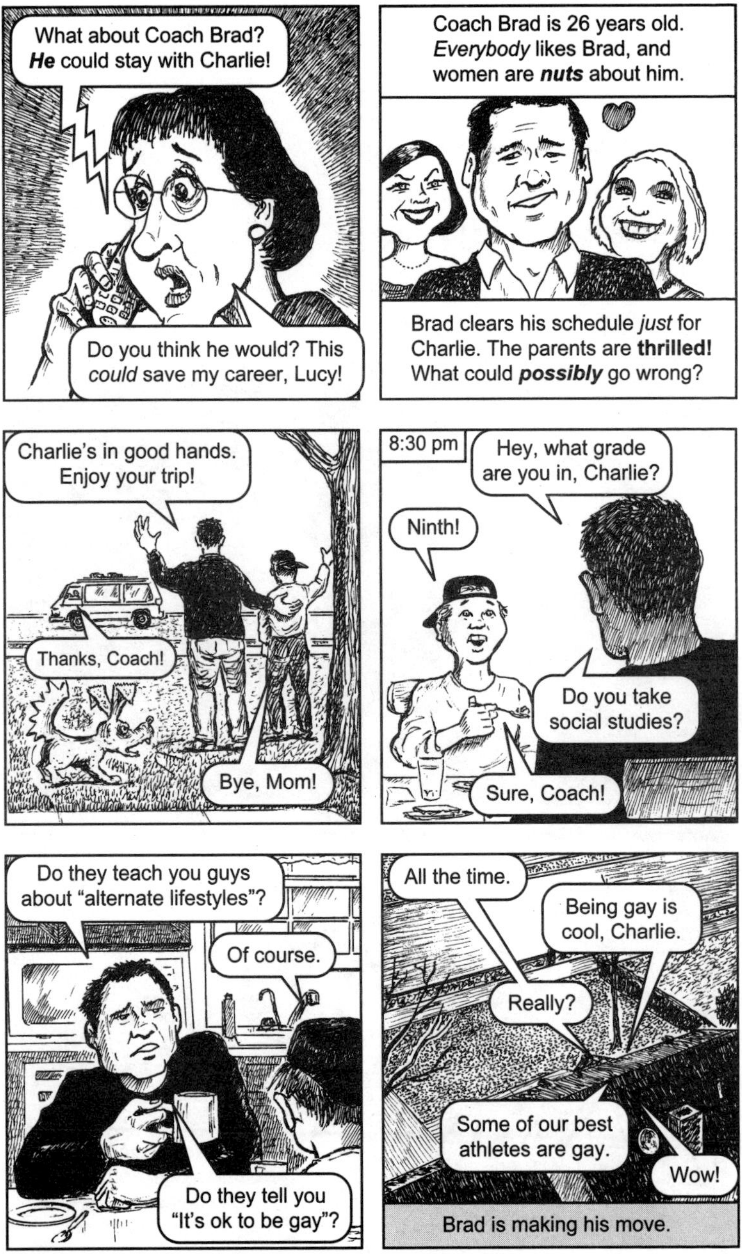
What about Coach Brad? *He* could stay with Charlie!
Do you think he would? This *could* save my career, Lucy!
Coach Brad is 26 years old. *Everybody* likes Brad, and women are ***nuts*** about him.
Brad clears his schedule *just* for Charlie. The parents are **thrilled!** What could ***possibly*** go wrong?
Charlie's in good hands. Enjoy your trip!
Thanks, Coach!
Bye, Mom!
8:30 pm
Hey, what grade are you in, Charlie?
Ninth!
Do you take social studies?
Sure, Coach!
Do they teach you guys about "alternate lifestyles"?
Of course.
Do they tell you "It's ok to be gay"?
All the time.
Being gay is cool, Charlie.
Really?
Some of our best athletes are gay.
Wow!
Brad is making his move.

They didn't **choose** to be gay, Charlie. They were **born** that way.

Oh?

Just like me!

Whoa! — Not true, Charlie!

Brad was *not* born that way.

At the age of 11, he was sent to juvenile hall for stealing. There he was raped by two older boys.

That act brought Brad into the homosexual world.

At midnight, Brad and Charlie watch late-night cable TV.

Just relax, Charlie.

GASP!

Charlie knows **nothing** about God or morals. His teachers were no help. He has **no defenses.**

To oppose the coach would be **"intolerant."** This made it easy for Brad to destroy his innocence.

The spirit that oppressed Brad now invaded Charlie.

Long before this happened, the stage had been set... ➡

The cry in our schools has been to defend the "downtrodden homosexuals."

What's the Day of Silence for?

Billy's Two Daddies

Yay!

For people to be "tolerant"... and for GLBT* kids to feel good!

The gays played the sympathy card...

*gay, lesbian, bisexual, transgender

...And it's paid off!

Intolerant Nazi *straight.*

You're a sick **homophobe.**

How *dare* you question our lifestyle?!

Like sheep, the crowd follows the current trend, which was brilliantly created by GLBT organizations.

Gay brainwashing floods our TV channels with gay sitcoms, gay news and gay films.

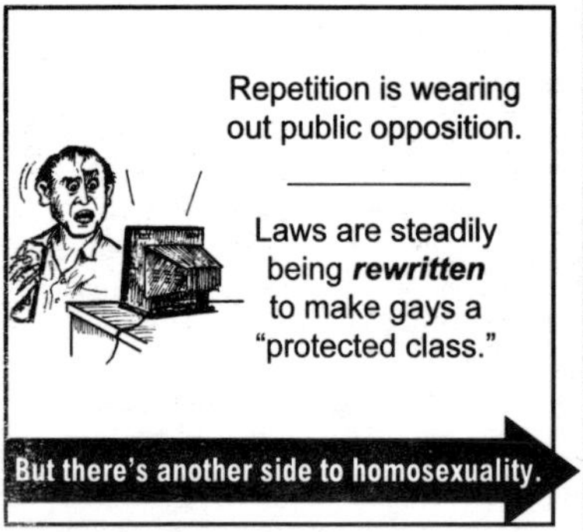
Repetition is wearing out public opposition.
Laws are steadily being ***rewritten*** to make gays a "protected class."
But there's another side to homosexuality.

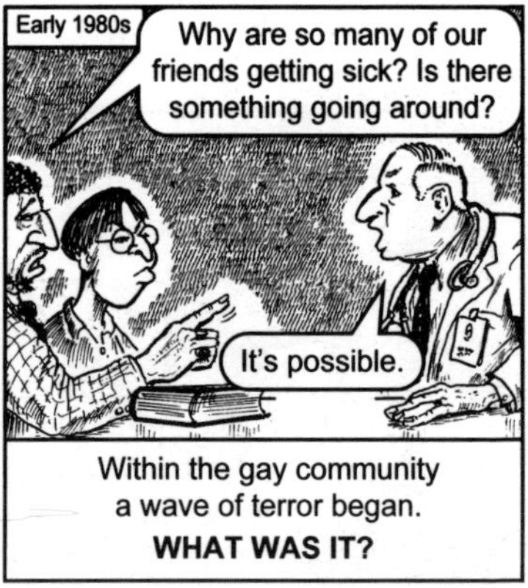
Early 1980s
Why are so many of our friends getting sick? Is there something going around?
It's possible.
Within the gay community a wave of terror began.
WHAT WAS IT?

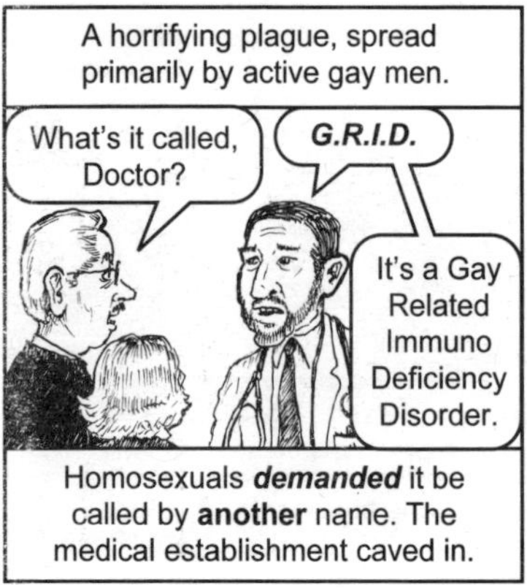
A horrifying plague, spread primarily by active gay men.
What's it called, Doctor?
G.R.I.D.
It's a Gay Related Immuno Deficiency Disorder.
Homosexuals ***demanded*** it be called by **another** name. The medical establishment caved in.

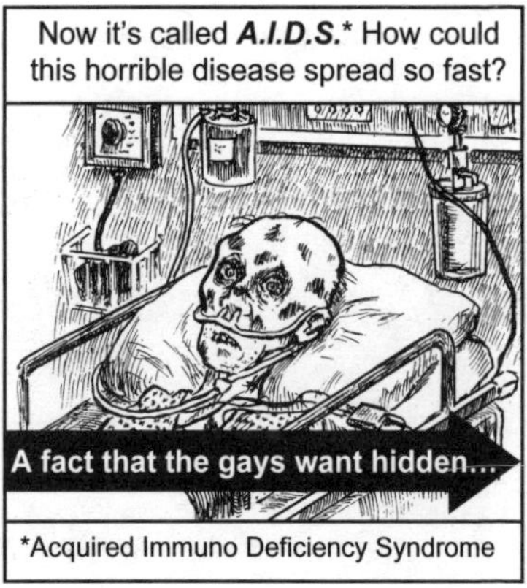
Now it's called ***A.I.D.S.**** How could this horrible disease spread so fast?
A fact that the gays want hidden...
*Acquired Immuno Deficiency Syndrome

A well-known study by Bell and Wineburg* showed that 43% of male homosexuals had over 500 sex partners during their lifetime.

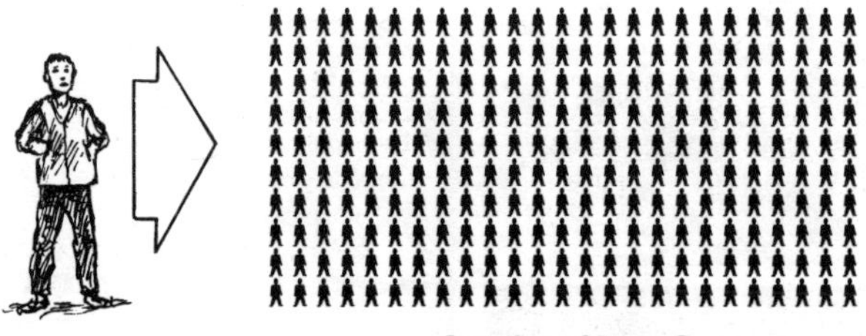

Get the picture?

* *"Homosexuality: A Study of Diversion Among Men and Women"* (Simon & Schuster, 1978), p. 308.

Homosexual perversion is everywhere in every nation, culture and neighborhood.

The gay community is at war with God. Their own churches pervert what He clearly said about homosexuality.

No wonder they're mad. See for yourself! ▶

After Noah's flood, perversion flourished in Babylonian religions and spread worldwide.*

Two of the worst cities were Sodom and Gomorrah. They were *exceedingly wicked.***

*See Babylon Religion (2006), available from Chick Publications.   **See Gen. 13:13

The Lord finally had enough. He pulled out the one righteous man (and his family) and then… **GOD'S JUDGMENT HIT!**

"Even as Sodom and Gomorrah, and the cities about them in like manner, giving themselves over to fornication, and going after strange flesh, are set forth for an example, suffering the vengeance of eternal fire." Jude 7

What does God say about homosexuality?

Nothing! He only talks about temple prostitutes or at worst, offensive gays.*

You really think so? You're in for a shock.

*This lie, "homosexual offenders," is found in 1 Cor. 6:9 in the New International Version (NIV).

Homosexuality is an *insult* to God. As He instructed Moses over 3,400 years ago:

"Thou shalt *not* lie with mankind, as with womankind: it is abomination." Lev. 18:22

God made it absolutely clear: *This* is a no-no!

To burn it into our brains, God spells it out:

"…Even their women did change the natural use into that which is *against* nature:"
Romans 1:26

Just Married

Also men, "...***Burned*** in their lust one toward another; men with men working that which is unseemly*..."
Romans 1:27

*Shameful, indecent

"Who knowing the judgment of God, that they which commit such things are worthy of death, not only do the same, but have pleasure in them that do them." Rom. 1:32

But what about Charlie?

Charlie is in shock. He's been *violated* by his trusted coach. He feels **dirty** and **ashamed**.

But if Charlie embraces the gay lifestyle…

His homosexual spirit will feed on others...

And his heart will harden against God.

Charlie needs to know that 2000 years ago, God put a plan in motion to set homosexuals free.

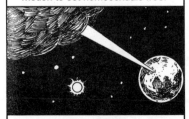

Jesus Christ, God the Son, was sent to earth for Charlie and for everyone else, because *we're all sinners.*

Jesus was **rejected**, *betrayed* by a close friend and **beaten**.

But why did God *take* all this abuse from sinful man?

Because *He loves us* — no matter **what we've done!**

Homosexuality
Backstabbing
Disobedient to parents
Haters of God
Whoremongers
Theft
Gossip   Pride
Guile
Cheating   Liars
Unmerciful
Anger   Envy
Lesbianism
Murder   Lust
Hypocrisy

"For God so loved the world, that he gave his only begotten Son, that whosoever believeth in him should not perish, but have everlasting life." John 3:16

"Who his own self bare our sins in his own body on the tree (cross), that we, being dead to sins, should live unto righteousness, by whose stripes ye were healed." 1 Peter 2:24

When *Brad* hears the gospel, he **rejects** it because his heart is hardened against God.

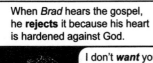

I don't **want** your "Jesus junk." I'm *happy* with my lifestyle.

"For the preaching of the cross is to them that perish foolishness..." 1 Cor. 1:18

But Charlie *still* feels the weight of guilt and responds…

If Jesus died for me, I want Him.

God the Holy Ghost tugs at Charlie's heart. What he does next will determine where he spends eternity.

Jesus, I believe You. Lord, come into my heart and clean up my life.

The unclean spirit leaves. Charlie's name is now in the Book of Life.

Years later Brad dies of complications from AIDS and stands before Jesus.

I shed my last drop of blood for **you**!

But you *spit* on my blood and *trampled* over my sacrifice.

To you it was worth **nothing**!

Is Brad's name in the *Book of Life*?

No, Lord, his name does **not** appear.

"**Depart** from me, ye cursed, into everlasting fire."*

*Matt. 25:41

Coach Brad joins all those who died in their sins.

The gossipers, liars, whoremongers, sodomites, haters of God, etc.*

But what happened to Charlie?

*Rom 1:29-32 and 1 Cor. 6:9-10

Charlie *was saved!*

"Enter thou into the joy of thy Lord."*

*Matt. 25:21

Gays are not **born** that way— they *choose* to be homosexuals.

God hates their lifestyle, and they oppose God.

Flee from it — or you'll pick up a devil that could ruin you for life.

Your *only* chance for heaven is Jesus. There's **no** other way.*

"…He that believeth *not*, is condemned already…"**

You must choose: Either Jesus Christ or the lake of fire.

"…Believe on the Lord Jesus Christ, and thou shalt be saved…"†

* John 14:6, ** See John 3:18, † Acts 16:31

THE BIBLE SAYS THERE'S ONLY ONE WAY TO HEAVEN!

Jesus said, "I am the way, the truth, and the life: no man cometh unto the Father, but by me." John 14:6

NOBODY ELSE CAN SAVE YOU. TRUST JESUS TODAY!

"That if thou shalt confess with thy mouth the Lord Jesus, and shalt believe in thine heart that God hath raised him from the dead, thou shalt be saved." Rom. 10:9

1. Admit you are a sinner. See Romans 3:10
2. Be willing to turn from sin (repent). See Acts 17:30
3. Believe that Jesus Christ died for you, was buried and rose from the dead. See Rom. 10:9-10
4. Through prayer, invite Jesus into your life to become your personal Saviour. See Rom. 10:13

WHAT TO PRAY

Dear God, I am a sinner and need forgiveness. I believe that Jesus Christ shed His **precious blood** and died for my sin. I am willing to turn from sin. I now invite Christ to come into my heart and life as my personal Saviour.

If you trusted Jesus as your Saviour, you have just begun a wonderful new life with Him. Now:

1. Read your Bible every day to get to know Jesus Christ better.
2. Talk to God in prayer every day.
3. Be baptized, worship, fellowship, and serve with other Christians in a church where Christ is preached and the Bible is the final authority.
4. Tell others about Jesus Christ.

Here's help to grow as a new Christian! Read **The Next Step**, available at Christian bookstores or from Chick Publications.

"They're out of the closet... and everybody is backing away." —JTC

~~~ HOME ALONE ~~~

JTC The aggressive homosexuals have built an army. They're on the offensive and they are showing no mercy or shame. It's unbelievable how they're moving into every area of our lives: our schools, entertainment, the political realm, the media.

They are "out of the closet," tooting their horns, and everybody is backing away. They give the impression that a high percentage of the population is homosexual. Actually it's around 2%.[1]

But they are very vocal and are making an impact. They even have their comedians pushing it. They get key people and high-class gay speakers, even on Fox and all the major networks. It's becoming a crime to even raise your eyebrow to say, "Whoops! You guys are taking away my civil rights!" That's enough to cause shockwaves. These guys are on the offensive. They are trying to use the word "pedophile" to cover up homosexual acts. Isn't that right, David?

---

1) So-called "experts" keep re-defining what it means to be a homosexual to inflate the numbers. This gives them political clout, so the lies continue. See David Kupelian, *The Marketing of Evil* (2005), cha. 1 & 6.

DWD That's true. They use different terms to confuse the public when talking about homosexuality in various places, like with the Boy Scouts and Catholic priests, for example. According to David Kupelian,[2] they say, "The Boy Scouts are not allowing 'homosexuals' as leaders." And they claim the kids are not in danger because "Homosexuals are never pedophiles."

On the other hand they are calling the priests who have abused altar boys for years "pedophile priests," not "homosexual priests." Yet the numbers clearly show that many of the young men that these priests have been abusing have already hit puberty. So it's *not* just pedophilia; that is *homosexual* abuse. But by only referring to them as "pedophiles," they are trying to hide the fact that those are really *homosexual* acts.

JTC In *Home Alone?* we expose the pressure tactics that homosexuals are using, as well as talk about sexually-transmitted diseases (STDs), the emotional scars and other problems that can result from this activity. And we're finding that these STDs are on the rise. In 2000 it was 1 in 4 people that were infected.

DWD Yes, and we are now closer to 1 in 3 people with at least one STD! And some of them are incurable. A 2008 report from the CDC[3] said that one in four girls ages 14-

---

2) David Kupelian is a Syrian Christian who is Managing Editor at WorldNetDaily.com, an independent news site, and author of *The Marketing of Evil: How Radicals, Elitists, and Pseudo-Experts Sell Us Corruption Disguised as Freedom* (WND Books, 2005).

3) Centers for Disease Control: www.cdc.gov.

19 has at least one of four major STDs —and two of them are incurable.[4]

JTC Back when AIDS first started to spread across the country, the medical establishment had to eliminate the *first* term they used for it —Gay-Related Immunodeficiency Disease (GRID).[5] The vast majority of the earlier cases were highly promiscuous male homosexuals. Under pressure they were forced to change it to Acquired Immune Deficiency Syndrome (AIDS).

Another problem with this AIDS thing came when Magic Johnson contracted HIV. Here he is, this great hero, and all the kids loved him. He was the star in the basketball world. Well, he's a multi-millionaire and he can afford all of the medication —the prices, they are astronomical— trying to keep that disease under control.

Kids on the street figure, "Well, so what? He didn't die, so I'm not going to die." And they don't even protect themselves. And this stuff keeps spreading. But when one dies, they don't say, "He died of AIDS;" instead they say, "He died of pneumonia—"

DWD Yes. It's because HIV (the Human Immunodeficiency Virus) eventually damages the immune system and shuts down

---

4) Human papillomavirus (HPV) and the STD form of herpes simplex virus. They may be treatable but not cured. See "Nationally Representative CDC Study Finds 1 in 4 Teenage Girls Has a Sexually Transmitted Disease," from the 2008 National STD Prevention Conference, March 10-13, 2008.

5) Or "Gay-Related Immune Deficiency" as stated in *Victory Deferred: How AIDS Changed Gay Life in America* by John-Manuel Andriote (1999), pp. 1, 50, 54, 213, and 220-21.

your body's ability to defend against these other viruses and bacteria. So what you die from is not AIDS *per se*. You die from what you caught while your defenses were down.

JTC We're trying to show kids (and their parents) to be careful who comes to your home, and who you are alone with. ***This story is a warning***. Yet we are up against all these "hate laws" while trying to speak about this issue.

The extreme attack that is coming out now is generally directed into the schools, from kindergarten up to college. Homosexuals cannot create babies, so they have to recruit. And our school kids are the target. The younger the better. State and federal lawmakers are approving this gay agenda, forcing teachers to promote it. David, you were working as a kindergarten teacher when the California education laws began to change.

DWD My district was able to hold it off for awhile. There were a lot of Christians and Catholics opposed to it. But ultimately the California school agenda said very clearly that teachers had to teach "alternative lifestyles."

Teachers are forced to reduce the time they teach reading, writing, math, social science and sciences, and instead teach children whatever "politically-correct" thing is currently being pushed. It is required that many kinds of perversion must be taught as "okay." They have to take hours out of the day and force students to watch plays about "tolerance" where they *show* kids all sorts of perversions, telling them they're "normal," "natural" and "healthy."

JTC Has this had an impact? You bet it has. Over half of the young people surveyed today think gay marriages are fine.[6]

DWD Secular media and public education[7] have worked very hard to change people's attitudes. And parents have little, if anything, to say about it. Recent court cases are increasingly handing power over our children to the state. Like children who believe that they're "oppressed" if they have to wait in line, now they're told they're "*re*pressed" if they don't gratify their every physical urge.

JTC That's why we wrote *Home Alone?* We know that new "hate laws" are being written to try to stop us, but we've *got* to sound the warning.

When we wrote this tract, we thought, "Man, who is going to pass this out? This thing is a "*hot topic!*" David had the idea of putting these *Hot Topics* in a single book so the reader can understand the reasoning behind these stories.

♦   ♦   ♦

6) *Seventeen* magazine polled teens in 1991 and 1999. The number of teenagers who accepted homosexuality as appropriate jumped from just 17% to 54%, over *three times* as many in only 8 years. See Kupelian, *The Marketing of Evil*, p. 32.

7) The film *It's Elementary* from Groundspark (www.groundspark.org), which teaches educators how to brainwash the kids into thinking homosexuality, lesbianism, etc., are normal lifestyles, has been shown in schools and churches since 1996. Small scenes are online on *YouTube* and other public outlets. Find out what your children are being taught!

"We're here. We're queer.
And we're coming after your children."[8]

WAKE UP! —

> *LOOK AROUND!* —

> > *TAKE ACTION!* —

Something horrible is happening! It is in our schools… on our television sets and our media. A full-scale war is being waged before our very eyes, and *your children* are the target! What you are about to read will shock you. But we have the opportunity to be part of the **solution**, so read on.

HOMOSEXUALS DON'T MOLEST CHILDREN, DO THEY?

Only about 2% of the people are homosexuals, yet *homosexuals perpetrate over one third of all reported child molestations*. Researchers Cameron and Coburn stated:

> "If 2% of the population [homosexual males] is responsible for 20% to 40% of something as socially and personally troubling as child molestation, *something must be desperately wrong with that 2%*."[9]

---

8) This was chanted during the 1993 Washington March for Gay Pride, according to Charles Socarides, MD, a clinical professor of psychiatry at Albert Einstein College of Medicine/Montefiore Medical Center in New York, president of the National Association for Research and Therapy of Homosexuality (NARTH), and author of *Homosexuality: A Freedom Too Far* (Phoenix, Arizona: Adam Margrave Books, 1995). Quote is from "How America Went Gay," *America* magazine, November 18, 1995.
9) See Paul Cameron and William Coburn, Jr., "Child Molestation and Homosexuality," *Psychological Reports* 58 (1986), pp. 327-337. Cited in *Press Bias and Politics: How the Media Frame Controversial Issues*, by Jim A. Kuypers (Praegers/Greenwood, 2002), p. 230. (Emphasis added.)

Homosexual activists point to the fact that annually more children are molested by heterosexual males than by gay males. But gays are only 2% of the population, so *a higher percentage* of them sexually abuse children. So while the number is *smaller*, the percentage of gay molesters is *higher*.

Harvard and Yale-connected psychiatrist Jeffrey Satinover summed it up this way:

> The greater absolute number of heterosexual cases reflects the fact that heterosexual males outnumber homosexual males by approximately 36 to 1. Heterosexual child molestation cases outnumber homosexual cases by only 11 to 1, implying that *pedophilia is more than three times more common among homosexuals*.[10]

WHY DO HOMOSEXUALS CARE ABOUT THE "AGE OF CONSENT?"

According to gay researchers Jay and Young, *73% of homosexuals surveyed have had sex at least once with boys 16-19 years old or younger*.[11]

In 2002 California Assemblyman Steve Baldwin wrote in a thoroughly-documented article for the *Regent University Law Review*:

> …the truth is stranger than fiction. Research confirms that homosexuals molest children at a rate vastly higher than heterosexuals, and the mainstream

10) *The Truth about Gay Pedophilia,* by Olivia St. John, *WorldNetDaily,* Oct. 7, 2006. (Emphasis added.)

11) *The Gay Report* by Karl Jay and Allen Young (New York: Summit Books, 1979), p. 275. (Emphasis added.)

homosexual culture commonly promotes sex with children. **Homosexual leaders repeatedly argue for the freedom to engage in consensual sex with children**, and blind surveys reveal a shockingly high number of homosexuals admit to sexual contact with minors. Indeed, **the homosexual community is driving the worldwide campaign to lower the legal age of consent.**[12]

> *"Scratch the average homosexual and you will find a pedophile."*[13]

Marxist and feminist Kate Millett made this clear as far back as 1980:

> Certainly, **one of children's essential rights is to express themselves sexually**, probably primarily with each other but *with adults as well*. So the sexual freedom of children is an important part of a sexual revolution.[14]

Her interviewer made it even clearer when he said:

> ...most gay male youth groups seem to support

---

12) *Child Molestation and the Homosexual Movement,* by Steve Baldwin, in the *Regent University Law Review* (2002), Vol. 14, No. 267, p. 268. (Emphasis added.)

13) Stated by South African homosexual and pedophile Kevin Bishop, who promoted the North American Man-Boy Love Association (NAMBLA) in an interview in the *Electronic Mail & Guardian* (June 30, 1997). Bishop was molested at the age of six and became a homosexual. See *Homosexual Activists Work to Normalize Sex with Boys,* Family Research Council publication, July 1999, p. 2.

14) From *Loving Boys,* Serniotext(e) Special, Intervention Series #2, Summer 1980. It also appeared in Daniel Tsang (Editor), *The Age Taboo: Gay Male Sexuality, Power and Consent* (Boston: Alyson Publications, 1981). (Emphasis added.)

> *lowering or abolition of the age of consent as a*
> *first step.*[15]

Lowering or abolishing the age of consent is a common theme in both gay and lesbian-oriented literature. But the trick is to make it *sound* like "children's rights," not what it really is: legal permission for pedophiles (male and female) to abuse children.

Millett also stated in the same interview:

> We have to have an emancipation proclamation for children. ***What is really at issue is children's rights and <u>not</u>, as it has been formulated up to now, <u>merely the right of sexual access to children</u>***.

OH YES IT IS! They want your children!

Did you know that most gay "travel guides" not only include lists of "gay-friendly" bars and hotels, but they also openly tell about the "age of consent" laws for that area? The message is clear: ***homosexuals are after <u>your</u>*** children.[16]

> ***Remember: gays don't reproduce;***
> ***they must recruit!***

Is all this campaigning working? Look at the lowering of the "age of consent" in the following chart and see for yourself. Remember: not so long ago all homosexual or lesbian

---

15) *Homosexual Activists Work to Normalize Sex with Boys*, Family Research Council publication (1999), lists other activists who state the same thing: the British homosexual group OutRage! (1998); the International Homophilics Institute (at least 1982-1997, the last date for which information was available); Pat Califa, author of *Sex with Boys* (1996); *Guide Magazine* (1995); the British homosexual group Stonewall campaigned for it (1992); the Second International Gay Youth Congress (1985), etc.
16) Gay travel guides are *much too filthy* to even reference.

relations were illegal in most countries. A lot has changed in the last few decades.

Summarized Age of Sexual Consent as of 2007[17]

Country	Male-Female	Male-Male (sodomy)	Female-Female
Australia	16-18[18]	16-18	16-17
Denmark	15	15	15
Italy	14	14	14
Japan	13[19]	13	13
Mexico	12-18[20]	12-18	12-18
UK	16-17[21]	16-18	16-17
USA	14-18	14-18[22]	14-18

HAS FREE SPEECH BECOME "HATE SPEECH?"

There is nothing subtle about the GLBT (gay, lesbian,

---

17) 2007 information was obtained from the AIDS charity, www.avert.org/aofconsent.htm. (Warning: this site is explicitly pro-GLBT.)

18) Varies by province.

19) Prefecture law can dictate 18 years of age.

20) Varies according to age gap between partners, and by regional law.

21) Varies by country. England, Scotland, Wales, Jersey and Isle of Man are 16; Northern Ireland is 17; Guernsey and Gibraltar are 18 for male-male and 16 for other contact. In 1994 Britain lowered the homosexual age of consent from 21 to 18. By 1998 it was lowered to 16, and that very year the government was urged to lower it to 14. Remember: they are never satisfied; they never stop. They are after your children!

22) Applies in 15 states; the current law regarding male-male or female-female sex was repealed or invalidated in 35 states and Washington D.C.

bisexual, transgender) agenda. It is everywhere: on television, movies, and in printed media. Christians do great harm to their kids when they look the other way and pretend it doesn't exist. We need to stay informed. David Kupelian wrote:

> The end game is not *only* to bring about the complete acceptance of homosexuality, including same-sex marriage, but also *to prohibit and even criminalize public criticism of homosexuality*, including the quotation of biblical passages disapproving of homosexuality."[23]

Did you notice? An ominous change has taken place. Criticism *in any form* has been redefined as "hate." That means Christians cannot criticize any belief or action without it being labeled "hate speech." But it's more than that. "Hate speech" is being written into the laws of cities, counties and states as if it were an actual crime.

To the GLBT lobby, disagreeing with them must be made *illegal.* Your free speech is a crime to them. These ungodly people are using the power of the law to close your mouth.

> *You or your children could be charged with a "hate crime" just for quoting what the Bible says about homosexuality!* [24]

Look carefully, and you will see that much of the "hate crimes" legislation is *really* about forcing jail time or other punishments on people who criticize homosexuality.

---

23) David Kupelian, *The Marketing of Evil* (2005), p. 35. (Emphasis added.)

24) You will learn more about "hate crimes" laws later in this book.

WHAT ARE THEY TEACHING MY CHILDREN?

• Did you know that school "Spirit Week" has been used as an excuse to have people cross-dress and be taught about "tolerance" of GLBT people?

They are after your children!

• Have you heard that one day each year in April has been dubbed the "Day of Silence?"[25] Students and teachers are silent for part of the day, then "speak out" about "anti-GLBT name-calling, bullying and harassment" and push a pro-GLBT agenda.

They are after your children!

• Were you aware that GLBT declared October to be "Coming Out Month," and that October 11th was designated "National Coming Out Day?" They encourage youth to "come out" as gay, lesbian, bisexual or transgender on that day to force the issue on families and pull young people caught in this trap into the GLBT "community."

They are after your children!

• Did you know that November 20 is called "Transgender Remembrance Day?"[26] As Christians we must recognize what is happening in our communities, right under our noses.

They are after your children!

---

25) A project developed by the Gay, Lesbian and Straight Education Network (GLSEN). In 2006 alone, over 4,000 colleges, high schools, middle schools and even elementary schools participated.

26) "Transgender Remembrance Day" is being pushed as a day "set aside to memorialize those who were killed due to anti-transgender hatred or prejudice (transphobia)." Note the use of the term "phobia" makes it *seem like biblical Christian beliefs are a psychological disorder.*

On October 12th 2007, laws were signed by California Governor Arnold Schwarzenegger forcing school curriculum to place a positive spin on GLBT people in discussions about sexuality in health, history and other classes.

As Harvard-educated homosexual writers Kirk and Madsen noted in *After the Ball*, their guide book for homosexual activism:

> Famous historical figures are considered especially useful to us for two reasons: first, they are invariably dead as a doornail, hence ***in no position ... to sue us for libel***. Second, and more serious, the virtues and accomplishments that make these historic gay figures admirable cannot be gainsaid or dismissed by the public, since ***high school history textbooks have already set them in incontrovertible cement***.[27]

In the public schools today, more and more children are being taught positive propaganda about homosexuality, bisexuality, lesbianism and other perversions in between. Schools throughout the nation encourage young people to "come out" and declare themselves to be gay, lesbian, bisexual or unsure of their gender.

How does it start? First, legislation masquerades itself as promoting "tolerance," but after the laws are passed, the story changes:

> Tolerance education is an important first step, but we need to push further.... Infuse LGBTQ cur-

---

27) *After the Ball: How America Will Conquer Its Fear and Hatred of Gays in the '90s* by Marshall Kirk and Hunter Madsen (New York: Penguin, 1989), p. 163. Quoted in *The Marketing of Evil* (2005), p. 28.

riculum into history, social science, and literature classes…[28]

Soon "tolerance" is no longer the issue. Recruiting your children is the next step. As more gay "counselors" come into the schools, they actively recruit your sons and daughters into "coming out" as a gay, lesbian, bisexual, or transgendered youth.

Programs like PROJECT 10 (a pro-GLBT organization founded by Dr. Virginia Uribe)[29] may have a "support system" in your child's school right now, promoting lies about homosexuality and pushing children to experiment in "alternate sexualities."

All these groups and counselors have one thing in common: telling your child to "experiment" with sexual and other perversions, in order to "find out" if he or she is GLBT —or something else.

WHAT CAN I DO?

One thing is for sure. As long as Christian parents and families continue to do nothing, the gay, lesbian, bisexual and transgender agendas will continue to erode your family's rights to free speech and to profess openly your belief in a holy God and that He calls these practices sins.

---

28) *Stripped bare: 'Gay' school plot unveiled*, by Bob Unruh, *WorldNetDaily*, Dec. 11, 2007. (Emphasis added.)

29) The name "Project 10" comes from the lie that 10% of the population is supposed to be homosexual. See *Crafting 'Gay' Children: An Inquiry into the Abuse of Vulnerable Youth via Government Schooling and Mainstream Media* by Judith A. Reisman Ph.D. (2001), p. 1.

Right now, waiting in the wings are the pedophiles ("inter-generational lovers") and others who ***badly want to have their way with your child***. The worst thing you can do is sit and do nothing.

If we don't act quickly,
we will lose our rights as parents and
legal protectors of our children.

HOW DO I START?

1. Stay aware and informed. Learn what is happening in your state, county, city and your child's school.

2. ***Talk to your children.*** They may know a lot more than they are telling you. They may even have been told by school officials *not* to tell you what is happening to them, inside the classroom and out.[30] Find out what *your* child is being taught and what the GLBT policies are in your school and school district.

3. Know who you are voting for and where they stand. The agenda of pro-gay office-seekers is out in the open nowadays. Make your vote count.

4. Pray for your community. Pray, pray, pray! We need wisdom to combat this perversion, directed at your child, disguised as "education."

5. Pass out gospel tracts. One of the quickest ways to spread the truth is through gospel tracts. They act as missionaries when you are gone, and they can be read time and

30) *District gags 14-year-olds after 'gay' indoctrination*, by Bob Unruh, *WorldNetDaily* March 13, 2007.

again. Only by a *real revival* can our communities and nation become a place of godly morality.

It only took a generation for things to get this bad. By pushing "gay education" in our schools and the media, the GLBT lobby has pushed their agenda that it's "okay" to pervert the use of our bodies. The situation is bleak, but there is hope.

You can be part of the solution! And this is the time to act! Don't hide in a corner. Inform *as many as you can* what God says about homosexuality: tell children, youth, adults and the elderly. ***They need to know!***

They're hammering at our kids through the media and education.

Christians have been afraid to touch the topic: But THEY are not afraid to touch our kids!

If you never tell your side, the GLBT lobby wins by default. So what do we do?

One Christian said:

> I make sure that, as I pass out or plant tracts, at least **one** of them is on the gay issue. That way, at least *one more person* has heard the other side. And if enough people hear, enough people can be persuaded to push aside the ungodly GLBT agenda —and prevent God's holy judgment!

Remember: The GLBT lobby is after your children!

"We shall sodomize your sons,
emblems of your feeble masculinity,
of your shallow dreams and vulgar lies.
We shall seduce them in your schools,
in your dormitories,
in your gymnasiums..."[31]

Glimpse of the (near) future?

---

31) Michael Swift in *Gay Community News*, February 15, 1987. Swift backtracked and claimed that his essay was "Outré, madness, a tragic, cruel fantasy, an eruption of inner rage, on how the oppressed desperately dream of being the oppressor." But wait a minute! Why would Michael Swift "desperately dream of being the **oppressor**"? This quote shows you how the gay community feels toward non-gay youth. Ask yourself: would you like this man's "inner rage" to erupt on *your* child?

America has been hit with a series of natural disasters that cost billions of dollars and have left people wondering, "What is happening?" But if we look at what happened *just before* the disaster, we begin to see a pattern. Could Somebody be angry?

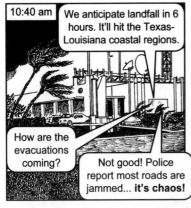

*National Severe Storm Laboratory

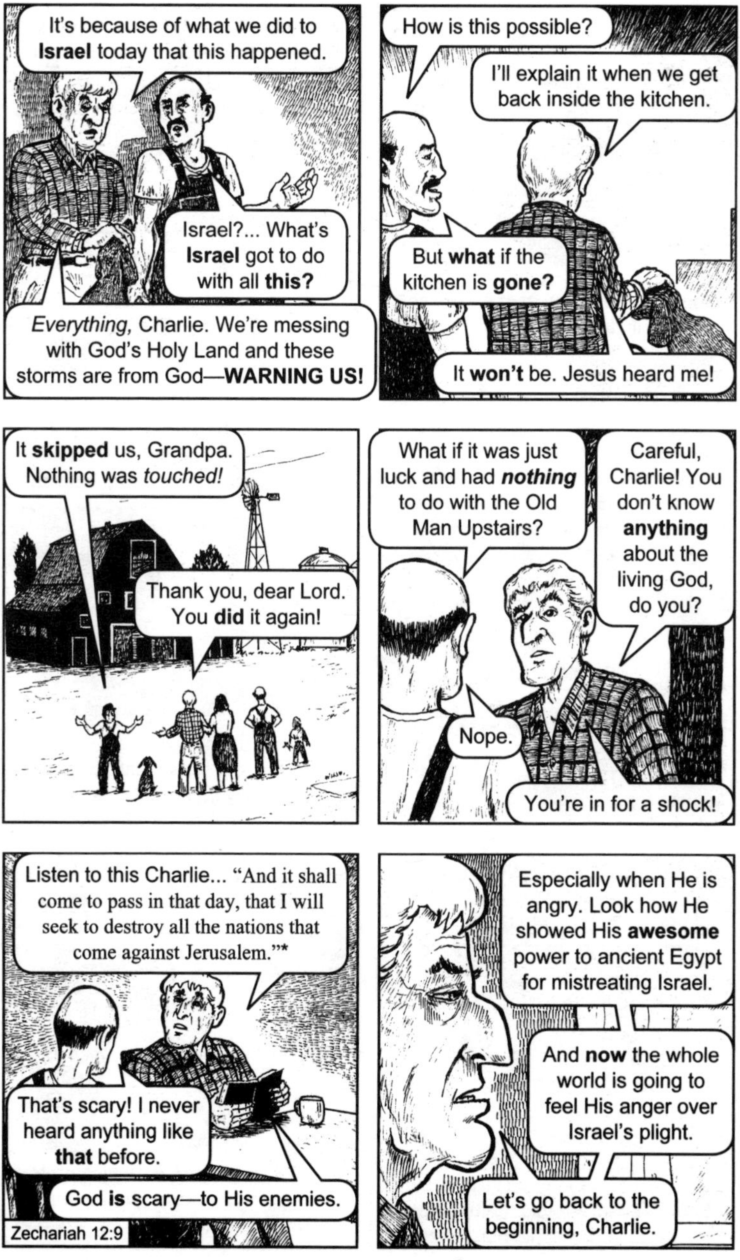
It's because of what we did to **Israel** today that this happened.
Israel?... What's **Israel** got to do with all **this?**
Everything, Charlie. We're messing with God's Holy Land and these storms are from God—**WARNING US!**
How is this possible?
I'll explain it when we get back inside the kitchen.
But **what** if the kitchen is **gone?**
It **won't** be. Jesus heard me!
It **skipped** us, Grandpa. Nothing was *touched!*
Thank you, dear Lord. You **did** it again!
What if it was just luck and had ***nothing*** to do with the Old Man Upstairs?
Careful, Charlie! You don't know **anything** about the living God, do you?
Nope.
You're in for a shock!
Listen to this Charlie... "And it shall come to pass in that day, that I will seek to destroy all the nations that come against Jerusalem."*
That's scary! I never heard anything like **that** before.
God **is** scary—to His enemies.
Zechariah 12:9
Especially when He is angry. Look how He showed His **awesome** power to ancient Egypt for mistreating Israel.
And **now** the whole world is going to feel His anger over Israel's plight.
Let's go back to the beginning, Charlie.

Out of the whole earth...

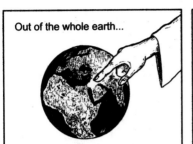

God chose one tiny spot for Himself. He calls it **"MY LAND."***

*2 Chronicles 7:19-22; Jeremiah 2:7; 16:18; Ezekiel 38:16-18; Joel 1:6-8; 3:2

And God chose one special family* to live on **His** land.

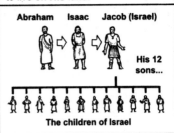

Abraham   Isaac   Jacob (Israel)

His 12 sons...

The children of Israel

*Joshua 21:43 "And the LORD gave unto Israel all the land which he sware to give unto their fathers; and they possessed it, and dwelt therein."

God called Israel's family "*His chosen people.*" When they suffered as slaves in Egypt... the Lord terrified the Egyptians. (See Exodus 5-11)

By the time they left, Egypt had been destroyed. Their crops, their wealth and their army were gone.

For 40 years God dwelt with them, feeding them manna from heaven.

God was with them as a cloud by day and a pillar of fire by night. God *never* did this to any other nation on earth.

God called Moses to lead His chosen people to the place that God calls *"My land."*

On the way, God gave His people laws to keep. He told them to obey His laws, so He could bless them.

When they got to the Promised Land, it was filled with nations greater and mightier than they. Even giants were there.

HAW HAW!

God said to drive them out and take the land for themselves... But *how?*

God went before them into battle and they were victorious. They called "God's Land" the nation of Israel.

Israel's borders went from the River of Egypt to the tip of the Euphrates River.

And the nation prospered. But then...

Israel **forgot** God, ignored His laws and *did evil.* So God gave them over to their enemies.

Lord, *save* us!

When they were sorry and begged Him to forgive them, God restored them, time after time.

They rebelled against God's laws* and were scattered across the world. They became known as the "Wandering Jew."

They were despised by society. **But the Holy Land *still* belongs to them.**

*Deuteronomy chapter 28

During World War II, Hitler murdered 6 million Jews. The whole world hated them — **especially** the Muslims, the Vatican and England.

It's God's **miracle** that Israel became a nation in 1948.

And the U.N. has hated them ever since.

England paid the price for double-crossing Israel. **She lost her Empire.**

I say, what happened to jolly old England?

Allahu akbar!

The Jews broke God's laws and paid the price, but the covenant stands! The Promised Land is theirs *forever.**

*Psalm 105:8-11; Jeremiah 31:35-37

All the world powers secretly want to please the Muslims by sacrificing Israel... for the sake of **oil**.

We blame Israel!

Woe to the nations that **dare** to mess with the land God calls **"MINE"**!

GOD IS ANGRY! ⟶

God's storms against America began in 1991.

President George H. W. Bush launched his *land-for-peace plan* by giving away Israeli land. *That day...*

God sent *The Perfect Storm* with 100 ft. waves into New England, damaging even President Bush's home.

In August 2005, the U.S. pressured Israel into evacuating Gaza. Families wept, losing **everything**.

Why?

While they **dug up** their dead* to re-bury them in *new* cemeteries, President George W. Bush applauded the dividing of God's land.

Was God pleased?

As America Has Done To Israel - McTernan pg. 213

The very next day, 8/29/05, a tropical depression formed. *Hurricane Katrina* pounded the U.S. — It became the largest disaster in U.S. history.

New Orleans was devastated. Over one million were forced from their homes, costing close to $200 billion.

When we mess with God's Holy Land, we pay the price.

The nations are insane! God's words warn us *not* to divide **His** land.

Israel has too much land.

But in their "push for peace," politicians are declaring war on the **same** God that demolished Ancient Egypt.

Here are the consequences.*

•**August 23, 1992:** Talks resume for Israel to surrender land for peace. Within 24 hours **Hurricane Andrew**, a "30-mile-wide tornado" slams the U.S. **Cost: $30 billion.**

•**April 27-September 13, 1993:** Israel and PLO work on and sign a compromise peace agreement in Washington D.C. During this same period the country is hit with the most devastating and widespread flooding in U.S. history. **Cost: $21 billion.**

•**Aug. 25-Sept 10, 2001:** The US, Arabia and Israel prepared the most comprehensive "peace plan" ever. God lifted His hand of protection, and the twin towers and Pentagon were attacked September 11th, *just before plans were finalized.* **Cost: Over $40 billion.**

•**November 7-12, 2002:** During Ramadan, President Bush hosted a dinner to honor Islam and the "revelation of God's word in the holy Koran" —*slapping the Living God in the face!* When officials flew to pressure Israel, 88 out-of-season tornadoes hit 7 states.

•**In 2005 alone**, messing with Israel cost the US **over $56 billion** in tornadoes, hurricanes, flood and drought.   **DOES ANYBODY NOTICE A PATTERN?**

*See *"Eye to Eye"* by William Koenig (2007)

Charlie, Jerusalem is God's **Holy City**. **Everybody** wants it: the Muslims, the popes and the United Nations.

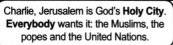

Jerusalem will be their undoing. Listen to God's warning:

"And in that day will I make Jerusalem a burdensome stone for all people: all that burden themselves with it shall be cut in pieces, though all the people of the earth be gathered together against it." Zechariah 12:3

God **will** unleash His fury against all nations and nothing will ever be the same. **Billions will die.**

All this happened because God made a promise to Abraham. But God has a **special** promise for *you*, Charlie.

What's that?

That **all** your sins can be forgiven and God will welcome you into heaven... *IF*...

...you put your faith in God's Son, Jesus Christ, and believe that He died on that cross as a sacrifice for your sins.

That's **all** I have to do to be saved?

Yes. The Lord Jesus died for your sins. He shed His precious blood, (God's blood)* to wash them away.   *Acts 20:28

"For God so loved the world, that he gave his only begotten Son, that whosoever believeth in him should not perish, but have everlasting life." John 3:16

3 days later Jesus rose from the dead. Israel's religious leaders turned their people against Him, *rejecting* God's love gift.

All unbelievers,* both Jew and Gentile, will die in their sins and go to hell.

Will you *reject* Jesus as **your** personal Saviour?

No, I don't *want* to go to hell! I want **Jesus.**

Then let's pray.

*John 3:17-18

Charlie received Jesus and was saved. The instant Charlie dies, he will be with his Saviour.

Very soon Jesus will return at the battle of Armageddon as Israel's Messiah. Only then will the surviving Jews respond to Him and be saved.

See Zechariah 12:10; Revelation 1:7.

When it is over, everyone born on this planet will bow before Jesus Christ, the King of Kings.*

"That at the name of Jesus every knee should bow, of things in heaven, and things in earth, and things under the earth; And that every tongue should confess that Jesus Christ is Lord, to the glory of God the Father." Philippians 2:10-11

*See Isaiah 45:23-25; Romans 14:11-12

Jesus will rule the world from Jerusalem. And Israel will have the land God promised them.

Do **you** want to reign with the Lord Jesus? You **will** if you receive Him as your personal Saviour.

This may be your **last** chance to decide...

Heaven or Hell... The choice is yours.

"...if thou shalt confess with thy mouth the Lord Jesus, and shalt believe in thine heart that God hath raised him from the dead, *thou shalt be saved*." Romans 10:9

THE BIBLE SAYS THERE'S ONLY ONE WAY TO HEAVEN!

Jesus said, "I am the way, the truth, and the life: no man cometh unto the Father, but by me." John 14:6

NOBODY ELSE CAN SAVE YOU. TRUST JESUS TODAY!

"That if thou shalt confess with thy mouth the Lord Jesus, and shalt believe in thine heart that God hath raised him from the dead, thou shalt be saved." Rom. 10:9

1. Admit you are a sinner. See Romans 3:10
2. Be willing to turn from sin (repent). See Acts 17:30
3. Believe that Jesus Christ died for you, was buried and rose from the dead. See Rom. 10:9-10
4. Through prayer, invite Jesus into your life to become your personal Saviour. See Rom. 10:13

WHAT TO PRAY

Dear God, I am a sinner and need forgiveness. I believe that Jesus Christ shed His **precious blood** and died for my sin. I am willing to turn from sin. I now invite Christ to come into my heart and life as my personal Saviour.

If you trusted Jesus as your Saviour, you have just begun a wonderful new life with Him. Now:

1. Read your Bible every day to get to know Jesus Christ better.
2. Talk to God in prayer every day.
3. Be baptized, worship, fellowship, and serve with other Christians in a church where Christ is preached and the Bible is the final authority.
4. Tell others about Jesus Christ.

Here's help to grow as a new Christian! Read **The Next Step**, available at Christian bookstores or from Chick Publications.

"God is really ticked off at America."
—JTC

~~~ SOMEBODY ANGRY? ~~~

JTC Even during this church age, God's attention is on His Holy Land. This is the land He gave to Abraham, and to his offspring. And it is still God's Holy Land.

The covenant with Israel still stands, regardless of how the Catholics or anyone else claims to be the "new Israel."[1] They say Israel rejected Christ, so they are out. But God still loves them, and they play a very important part in the future. They are still God's chosen people, even though they are in rebellion.

We have to pray for Israel, and we have got to bless Israel. We must "pray for the peace of Jerusalem."[2] But the leaders of this world are in complete rebellion. Read Psalm 2:

> Why do the heathen rage, and the people imagine a vain thing? The kings of the earth set themselves, and the rulers take counsel together, against the LORD, and against his anointed...[3]

---

1) This is called "Replacement Theology."
2) See Psalm 122:6: "Pray for the peace of Jerusalem: they shall prosper that love thee."
3) Psalm 2:1-3.

41

They are fooling around with Jerusalem, God's property. He gave it to the Jews and now the USA and UN are saying, "Hey, we are going to divide up the land." And if you divide that land up, God has marked your nation as a target.

DWD It used to be said, "The sun never sets upon the British empire." But *their* sun set as soon as they double-crossed the nation of Israel.[4]

JTC And what happens to nations who rebel against the Lord Jesus? Look at Psalm 2:9:

> Thou shalt break them with a rod of iron; thou shalt dash them in pieces like a potter's vessel.

At His Second Coming, He is not going be the "gentle Jesus" we saw during His lifetime.

DWD

> Kiss the Son, lest he be angry, and ye perish from the way, when his wrath is kindled but a little…[5]

JTC Our leaders are not fearful; they do not tremble over the word of God. They ignore it completely. Therefore the United Nations is going down. And God is going to hit **us** because we are messing with Jerusalem and His Holy Land. The Lord is already flexing His muscles.

We have the same God who brought the children of Israel out of Egypt. God is alive and well, and He is really ticked off at America. We have *ignored* His command to bless Jerusalem and we *dare* to pressure Israel to give away

---

4) See the tract, "Love the Jewish People," pp. 10-14.
5) Psalm 2:12.

His land to His enemies. Do you think God is going to put up with it?

DWD Many people seem to think the most important verse about Jewish people is Romans 10:21:

> But to Israel he saith, All day long I have stretched forth my hands unto a ***disobedient and gainsaying people***.

Then they close the book and say, "See? That is the end of Israel." But the very next verses say:

> I say then, Hath God cast away his people? ***God forbid***... God hath ***not*** cast away his people which he foreknew.[6]

JTC The covenant stands. We did *Somebody Angry?* to show the reader what we've gotten ourselves into. Look what we are doing to His chosen people. We'd better "batten down the hatches; the big storm is coming" because our leaders are *not* going to change. They are *determined* to set up a separate state in Israel: one state for the Muslims and one for Israel.

This is going to be our undoing. The storms that are hitting us are only a foretaste of the wrath of God against us for rejecting His people and His land.

DWD On every side but the Mediterranean Sea they are surrounded by Muslims. So why are Muslims so desperate to take this itty bitty little piece of land that is only 30 miles across and divide it in half?

---

6) Romans 11:1-2.

JTC Because Satan *hates* the Jewish people.

DWD And he will stop at nothing to get nations—even Christians—to pull away all support from them. But they risk the wrath of God.

Here are some books we recommend:

- Eye to *Eye: Facing the Consequences of Dividing Israel,* by William Koenig[7]
- *As America Has Done to Israel* by John P. McTernan[8]
- *God's Final Warning to America* by John P. McTernan[9]
- *Israel: A Deadly Piece of Dirt* by Peter S. Ruckman[10]

◆　　◆　　◆

AMERICA'S WARNING SHOT FROM HEAVEN

God spoke America's warning shot from heaven very plainly:

> The burden of the word of the LORD for Israel, saith the LORD… Behold, I will make Jerusalem a cup of trembling unto all the people round about… And in that day will I make Jerusalem a burdensome

---

7) Alexandria, Virginia: About Him Publishing, 2007.

8) Xulon Press, 2006.

9) Oklahoma City, Oklahoma: Hearthstone Publishing, 1996, 1998, 2000.

10) Pensacola, FL: Bible Believers Bookstore, 2001.

stone for all people: all that burden themselves with it shall be cut in pieces, though all the people of the earth be gathered together against it.[11]

What is the point of this scripture? It's simple: You don't want to mess with God's land.

WHAT CAN I DO?

• "Pray for the peace of Jerusalem."[12]

• Pray for your elected leaders,[13] that they never fall to the fatal temptation of abandoning Israel.

• Pass out this tract.

• Tell your family members and friends about what God thinks about Israel. As you educate others on this issue, they will educate their legislators.

• Vote what you believe.

• Keep your elected representatives accountable.

• Spread this message in your church.

As God's people become more aware and pray for Israel, perhaps God may turn away His wrath against this country for one more generation.

---

11) Zechariah 12:1-3.
12) Psalm 122:6.
13) 1 Timothy 2:1-4.

Religious and political leaders tell us that Allah is the same as the Christian God. But the Qur'an insists no less than *18 times* that, unlike the God of the Bible, Allah never had a Son! Who, then, *is* Allah? And why should I care about Allah or Islam?

ALLAH HAD NO SON

J.T.C.

47

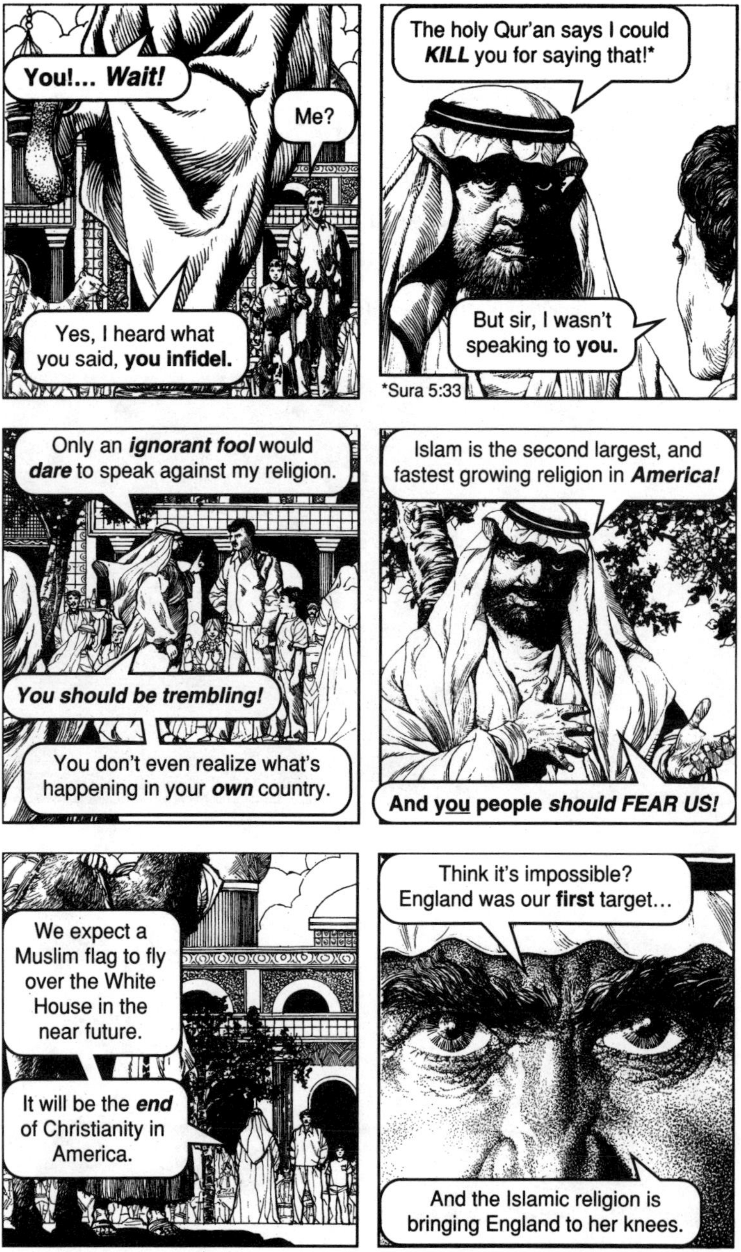
You!... *Wait!*
Me?
Yes, I heard what you said, **you infidel.**
The holy Qur'an says I could ***KILL*** you for saying that!*
But sir, I wasn't speaking to **you.**
*Sura 5:33
Only an ***ignorant fool*** would ***dare*** to speak against my religion.
You should be trembling!
You don't even realize what's happening in your ***own*** country.
Islam is the second largest, and fastest growing religion in ***America!***
And you people *should FEAR US!*
We expect a Muslim flag to fly over the White House in the near future.
It will be the ***end*** of Christianity in America.
Think it's impossible? England was our **first** target...
And the Islamic religion is bringing England to her knees.

You are a Christian, correct?

Yes, sir.

You **infidels** should **know** that your Bible is corrupt…

because the Holy Qur'an **condemns** it.

No man who ever **lived** was greater than Muhammad…

Blessings be upon him.

Muhammad **was innocent,** and the **greatest** of prophets.

He gave us the blessed **Qur'an.**

CHRISTIANITY IS A LIE!

And Jesus, the **Jew,** was **never** crucified.

Islam truthfully teaches that **SOMEONE ELSE** died on the cross.*

* *Anatomy of the Qur'an* by Moshay, pp. 98-101.

And Jesus **can't** be God's Son because the Qur'an declares, "SAY NOT THAT ALLAH BEGOT A SON."*

That's no problem, sir, because Allah is **NOT** God!

Gasp!

*Sura 23:91

History proves that **before** Islam came into existence…

The Sabeans in Arabia worshiped **the moon god**…

…who married the **sun goddess,** who gave birth to **three** goddesses.

They were called Al-lat, Al-uzza and Manat. They later became **idols**…

and were **worshipped** throughout that part of the world as the **"Daughters of Allah."**

My friend, the moon god was **Allah**.

The crescent moon is everywhere in Islam.

Even Ramadan begins and ends with the crescent moon.

He was just **one** of 360 **idols** in the Ka'aba* in Mecca.

Ask your mullah why!

And Muhammad *knew* all about this.

It's not good to ask such questions.

*Islam's holy house of god

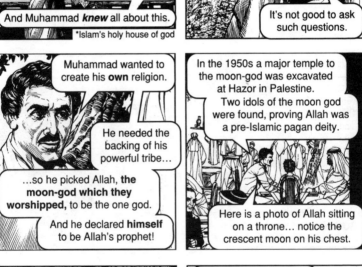

Muhammad wanted to create his **own** religion.

In the 1950s a major temple to the moon-god was excavated at Hazor in Palestine.

He needed the backing of his powerful tribe…

Two idols of the moon god were found, proving Allah was a pre-Islamic pagan deity.

…so he picked Allah, **the moon-god which they worshipped,** to be the one god.

And he declared **himself** to be Allah's prophet!

Here is a photo of Allah sitting on a throne… notice the crescent moon on his chest.

See *Islamic Invasion* by Dr. Robert A. Morey, pp 211-218.

So now you see that on the day of judgement…

YOU and all **Muslims** will be trembling. You have been betrayed!

But there is a **real** God in heaven who **died for all Muslims** and wants them to know the **truth.**

He is God the Father, God the Son, and God the Holy Ghost.

These three are the **one true God.***

*1 John 5:7

Jesus Christ, the only begotten Son of the living God, **created the universe.** Rev. 4:11

Every Muslim living today is breathing because Jesus Christ gave them life… and they don't even know Him.

The Word of God says:

"All things were made by him (Jesus); and without him was not anything made that was made…" John 1:3

"He was in the world, and the world was made by him, and the world knew him not." John 1:10

Jesus Christ will judge* all who ever lived. On the last day Muhammad will bow down and say…

Jesus Christ is Lord! **

*John 5: 27   **Philippians 2:11

(Gasp) If this is true then I have no hope!

My friend, if you should die tonight, who's going to help you in eternity?

Because of sin, the gates of heaven are closed. God will not allow sin in His presence.

But God in His mercy made a way for all people, including the precious Muslims, to get rid of their sins.

He sent God the Son, Jesus Christ, from heaven to die for our sins.*

*1 John 4:14

Because God loves the lost people of Islam He wants them to live with Him in mansions in heaven.

Beloved, the truth is that Allah is **not God**, Muhammad was **no prophet** and the Qur'an is **not the Word of God.***

See *Christ, Muhammad and I* by Mohammad Al Ghazoli.

When God the Holy Ghost came upon the virgin Mary, she conceived and bore the sinless Christ. (Luke 1:35)

Mary was blessed and later had other children by her husband, Joseph. (Mark 6:3)

Later in his public ministry Jesus said,

"I am the way, the truth, and the life:

no man cometh unto the Father (in heaven), but by me."*

*John 14:6

At the crucifixion the Lord Jesus Christ shed His precious, holy blood to wash away your sins… to give you eternal life in heaven. (Rev. 1:5)

"For God so loved the world (you), that he gave his only begotten Son (Jesus) that whosoever believeth in him should not perish (in hell), but have everlasting life (in heaven)." John 3:16

On this day alone, Jesus fulfilled over 30 prophecies when the Creator allowed Himself to be murdered by man.

It is finished!

"He is despised and rejected of men; a man of sorrows, and acquainted with grief: and we hid as it were our faces from him; he was despised, and we esteemed him not... But he was wounded for our transgressions, he was bruised for our iniquities: the chastisement of our peace was upon him; and with his stripes we are healed." Isaiah 53:3,5

Jesus died, was buried and rose from the dead three days later. He is now at the right hand of the Father in heaven, and is coming again soon in power and great glory.

After His resurrection, the Lord Jesus appeared in His glory to His apostle John and said:

"I am he that liveth, and was dead; and, behold, I am alive for evermore...

and have the keys of hell and of death."
Rev. 1:18

If all this is true, how can I be saved from hell?

Recognize that Satan has deceived you.

Admit that you are a sinner in need of a Saviour, repent, and ask Jesus to come into your heart.

O God, I've been deceived. Allah is a false god, Muhammed is not your prophet and the Qur'an is not Your Holy Word.

I trust You as my Saviour. Come into my heart, Lord Jesus.

For more of the truth about Islam,
See *Who Is This Allah?* by G.J.O. Moshay, available from Chick Publications.

THE BIBLE SAYS THERE'S ONLY ONE WAY TO HEAVEN!

Jesus said, "I am the way, the truth, and the life: no man cometh unto the Father, but by me." John 14:6

NOBODY ELSE CAN SAVE YOU.
TRUST JESUS TODAY!

"That if thou shalt confess with thy mouth the Lord Jesus, and shalt believe in thine heart that God hath raised him from the dead, thou shalt be saved." Rom. 10:9

1. Admit you are a sinner. See Romans 3:10
2. Be willing to turn from sin (repent). See Acts 17:30
3. Believe that Jesus Christ died for you, was buried and rose from the dead. See Rom. 10:9-10
4. Through prayer, invite Jesus into your life to become your personal Saviour. See Rom. 10:13

WHAT TO PRAY

Dear God, I am a sinner and need forgiveness. I believe that Jesus Christ shed His **precious blood** and died for my sin. I am willing to turn from sin. I now invite Christ to come into my heart and life as my personal Saviour.

If you trusted Jesus as your Saviour, you have just begun a wonderful new life with Him. Now:

1. Read your Bible every day to get to know Jesus Christ better.
2. Talk to God in prayer every day.
3. Be baptized, worship, fellowship, and serve with other Christians in a church where Christ is preached and the Bible is the final authority.
4. Tell others about Jesus Christ.

Here's help to grow as a new Christian! Read **The Next Step**, available at Christian bookstores or from Chick Publications.

"If they pull this off, we are dead meat!"
—JTC

⌇⌇ ALLAH HAD NO SON ⌇⌇⌇⌇⌇⌇⌇⌇⌇⌇⌇⌇⌇⌇⌇

DWD Why are Muslims so infuriated at the tract *Allah Had No Son?*

JTC When I worked with Alberto Rivera on *The Prophet*,[1] he explained how the Vatican created this new "daughter," Islam, to pull all the Bedouins together into one religion that the Vatican could eventually control.

As a byproduct of that, I wanted to make sure that the American public, and everyone else, got some insight into Islam. It's nothing like we are told by the media. This monster is a very sinister, evil force. If and when it comes into power here in the US, we are *dead meat!*

DWD Why did you pick *Allah Had No Son* as the title?

JTC Because in parts of the world, people's Bibles read:

For ***Allah*** so loved the world that he gave his only begotten son...[2]

---

1) *The Prophet* is Crusaders magazine #16, also known as Alberto #6, available from Chick Publications.

2) For example, a translation otherwise seen as very accurate, the *Van Dyke* Arabic Bible, uses the word *Allah* for God. This makes it much harder for the people to understand that Allah is **not** God!

55

That was *mandated* by the local governments when the Bible was being translated in these Arab countries. They *had* to call God "Allah" —by *that* name.

Muhammad had said in the Qur'an, "Allah had no son."[3] But when the Christians **have** to use the word "Allah," their work has already been sabotaged.

DWD Muslims are taught all their lives from their authority, the Qur'an, that Allah is unknowable, that he doesn't love mankind, and that he never had a son, much less one that was sent to the cross.

So when Christians say that Allah is God, Muslims think, "How silly! **Everyone** knows that Allah had no son." The Muslims have sabotaged the Christian witness by getting us to say that our God is Allah.

What would happen if you started calling God "Baal," "Molech" or "Ishtar?" Do you think God would bless your missionary effort or your Bible? Or would He be deeply offended at such blasphemy? That's no different from calling Him the name of a tiny Middle Eastern moon god idol that was worshiped by Muhammad's tribe, but that's exactly what people are doing.

JTC Dr. Rivera described to me the creation of Islam and its development by the Catholic system. I was absolutely stunned when I learned how it came about. And I realized that that information had to go into a Crusaders story that reveals the entire operation. We called it *The Prophet*.

---

3) See the documentation at the end of this chapter.

The Vatican and top Islamic leaders know what took place. But it's covered up.

Allah Had No Son was a breakthrough tract for people on the street. The main issues of Islam were made simple. It's been out since the mid-90's, but it needs to be spread even more because when the President told us that Islam is a peaceful religion, he was completely off-the-wall. But the vast majority of people bought it.

DWD It is interesting that this wasn't said until *after* 9/11, when Muslims crashed planes into the World Trade Center and the Pentagon and aimed a fourth plane at Washington. How ironic: Muslims, faithfully following the Qur'an, commit the worst devastation ever to happen to this country, and *then* leaders say, "Islam is a **peaceful** religion!"

The president, not wanting to anger our Arab oil suppliers and see our oil supplies dry up, wouldn't say anything *negative* about Islam. Instead, he made a statement that denies basic Islamic teaching, and the Qur'an itself.

Maybe he was just listening to his counselors and speech writers, but the damage was done. It became *politically incorrect* to say a word against the violence of Islam, much less Muhammad, Allah or the Qur'an.

JTC Yes, and now some schools are teaching kids to celebrate Ramadan, dress in Islamic clothing, call themselves by Islamic names and memorize verses out of the Qur'an. It's insanity! But even more, this shows the impending **danger** of Islam's growing influence here in the US.

DWD Moshay, in his book *Who Is This Allah?* tells how in

1980, the US Congress decided to "congratulate Islam for its 14 centuries of existence." Then the National Council of Churches "sent a congratulatory message" to all the Muslim organizations in America. Moshay said that:

> Immediately after this anniversary and the pledge for support that Islamic leaders received from the government and "the church," Islam began to grow in the U.S. Many more Muslims began flooding America to study and to settle down. They had feared that, if they went to America, they would be converted to Christianity. But that fear was removed. [4]

JTC They're getting more publicity now than Catholicism. But they're tied together. This is the scary part of it. Our job is to warn everybody that this Allah, who everybody is saying is our God, is *not* our God. Allah is a moon god idol, backed by a devil out of hell.

DWD Yes, like it says in the Psalms:

> For all the gods of the nations are idols: but the LORD made the heavens.[5]

JTC And all these poor Muslims are headed straight for the pit. Somebody's got to stand up for the living God and warn them. God gave us the story and we published it. Why? Because we don't want them to go to hell.

DWD If you say that Allah is the living God, then you are

---

4) *Who Is This Allah?* by G.J.O. Moshay (2008), p. 78. Available from Chick Publications.

5) Psalm 96:5. For more on who Allah really is, see *Who Is This Allah?* and *Christ, Muhammad and I,* available from Chick Publications.

caught in their trap, like all the other nations that have fallen to Islam. And you cannot placate Islam.

JTC Muslims have said for years that the flag of Islam will one day fly over the White House. We cannot escape the fact that the US is a target —a **major** target. They know that if they pull us down, they have got the world.

DWD They desperately need the gospel. And our tract, *Allah Had No Son,* shows them the gospel, as well as who Allah really is. We need soul winners who will love them enough to give them this tract.

◆   ◆   ◆

THE LITTLE BEDOUIN IDOL
WHO WOULD BE GOD

The Bible declares that Jesus is the Son of God.[6] If the Qur'an says that Jesus is NOT Allah's son, then Allah and God are not the same. Let's see what the Qur'an says:

*Please note that all Qur'an verses are from the Yusuf Ali translation, unless otherwise noted.

Sura 2:116...

They say: "Allah hath begotten a son": Glory be to Him.-Nay, to Him belongs all that is in the heavens and on earth: everything renders worship to Him.

Summary: Allah had no son.

Sura 6:101...

To Him is due the primal origin of the heavens and the earth: How can He have a son when He hath no consort? He created all things, and He hath full knowledge of all things.

Summary: Allah cannot have a son because he has no consort.

Sura 9:30...

The Jews call 'Uzair [Ezra] a son of Allah, and the Christians call Christ the son of Allah. That is a saying from their mouth; (in this) they but imitate

---

6) See Mark 1:1; Luke 1:35; John 1:34; 3:18; 9:35-38; 10:36; 20:31; Acts 8:37; 9:20; 2 Corinthians 1:19; Hebrews 4:14; 1 John 4:15; 5:5; 5:10, 12-13, 20 and other scriptures.

what the unbelievers of old used to say. Allah's curse be on them: how they are deluded away from the Truth.

Summary: Allah's curse on those who say Christ is Allah's son.

Sura 9:31...

They take their priests and their anchorites to be their lords in derogation of Allah, and (they take as their Lord) Christ the son of Mary; yet they were commanded to worship but One Allah: there is no god but He. Praise and glory to Him: (Far is He) from having the partners they associate (with Him).

Summary: People should not take Christ as their Lord —they should only worship Allah. There is no Godhead, only Allah.

Sura 10:68...

They say: "Allah hath begotten a son!" - Glory be to Him! He is self-sufficient! His are all things in the heavens and on earth! No warrant have ye for this! say ye about Allah what ye know not?

Summary: Allah had no son. It is ignorant to say he did.

Sura 17:111...

Say: "Praise be to Allah, who begets no son, and has no partner in (His) dominion: Nor (needs) He any to protect Him from humiliation: yea, magnify Him for His greatness and glory!"

Summary: Allah had no son and there is no Godhead.

Sura 18:4-5...

Further, that He may warn those (also) who say, "Allah hath begotten a son": No knowledge have they of such a thing, nor had their fathers. It is a grievous thing that issues from their mouths as a saying what they say is nothing but falsehood!

Summary: Allah had no son. It is ignorance and a lie to say he did.

Sura 19:35...

It is not befitting to (the majesty of) Allah that He should beget a son. Glory be to Him! when He determines a matter, He only says to it, "Be", and it is.

Summary: Allah does not need to beget a son. He can create what he wants.

Sura 19:88-95...

They say: "(Allah) Most Gracious has begotten a son!" Indeed ye have put forth a thing most monstrous! At it the skies are ready to burst, the earth to split asunder, and the mountains to fall down in utter ruin, That they should invoke a son for (Allah) Most Gracious. For it is not consonant with the majesty of (Allah) Most Gracious that He should beget a son. Not one of the beings in the heavens and the earth but must come to (Allah) Most Gracious as a servant. He does take an account of them (all), and hath numbered them (all) exactly. And every one of them will come to Him singly on the Day of Judgment.

Summary: It is a monstrous thing to say Allah had a son. Jesus was just a servant, and Jesus will also be judged by Allah on Judgment Day.

Sura 21:26...

And they say: "(Allah) Most Gracious has begotten offspring." Glory to Him! they are (but) servants raised to honour.

Summary: Allah had no son, only a servant raised to honor.

Sura 23:91...

No son did Allah beget, nor is there any god along with Him: (if there were many gods), behold, each god would have taken away what he had created, and some would have lorded it over others! Glory to Allah! (He is free) from the (sort of) things they attribute to Him!

Summary: Allah had no son, and there is no Godhead. Muslims mistakenly think the Trinity means three gods, not one God in three persons.[7]

Sura 25:2...

He to whom belongs the dominion of the heavens and the earth: no son has He begotten, nor has He a partner in His dominion: it is He who created all things, and ordered them in due proportions.

Summary: Allah had no son, and there is no Godhead.

---

7) See 1 John 5:7-8 (KJV).

Sura 31:13 (Pickthal)…

And (remember) when Luqman said unto his son, when he was exhorting him: O my dear son! Ascribe no partners unto Allah. Lo! to ascribe partners (unto Him) is a tremendous wrong –

Summary: It is a tremendous wrong to have a Godhead. Allah is alone.

Sura 37:152…

Is it not that they say, from their own invention, "Allah has begotten children"? but they are liars!

Summary: Only liars say that Allah begat anyone.

Sura 39:4…

Had Allah wished to take to Himself a son, He could have chosen whom He pleased out of those whom He doth create: but Glory be to Him! (He is above such things.) He is Allah, the One, the Irresistible.

Summary: Allah had no son. If he wanted one, he could have picked one of his creations to be his son. But he didn't.

Sura 43:81…

Say: "If (Allah) Most Gracious had a son, I would be the first to worship."

Summary: Muhammad would be the first to worship Allah's son.

Sura 72:3…

And Exalted is the Majesty of our Lord: He has taken neither a wife nor a son.

Summary: Allah had no wife and had no son.

Sura 112:1-3...

> Say: He is Allah, the One and Only; Allah, the Eternal, Absolute; He begetteth not, nor is He begotten; And there is none like unto Him.

Summary: Allah is the "one and only" and there is none like him.[8]

WHAT DOES THE QUR'AN CALL "BLASPHEMY?" (AN INSULT TO ALLAH)

Sura 5:1...

> In blasphemy indeed are those that say that Allah is Christ the son of Mary. Say: "Who then hath the least power against Allah, if His will were to destroy Christ the son of Mary, his mother, and all every - one that is on the earth? For to Allah belongeth the dominion of the heavens and the earth, and all that is between. He createth what He pleaseth. For Allah hath power over all things."

Summary: It is blasphemy to say that Christ is Allah.

Sura 5:72...

> They do blaspheme who say: "Allah is Christ the son of Mary." But said Christ: "O Children of Israel! worship Allah, my Lord and your Lord." Whoever

---

8) Strangely, calling Allah the "One and Only" matches the NIVs perverted reading of John 1:18 ("God the One and Only" instead of the correct "only begotten Son.")

joins other gods with Allah,-Allah will forbid him the garden, and the Fire will be his abode. There will for the wrong-doers be no one to help.

Summary: It is blasphemy to say that Christ is Allah.

Sura 5:73...

They do blaspheme who say: Allah is one of three in a Trinity: for there is no god except One Allah. If they desist not from their word (of blasphemy), verily a grievous penalty will befall the blasphemers among them.

Summary: It is blasphemy to say that Allah is part of the Trinity. Allah is alone.

Sura 6:19...

Say: "What thing is most weighty in evidence?" Say: "Allah is witness between me and you; This Qur'an hath been revealed to me by inspiration, that I may warn you and all whom it reaches. Can ye possibly bear witness that besides Allah there is another Allah?" Say: "Nay! I cannot bear witness!" Say: "But in truth He is the one Allah, and I truly am innocent of (your blasphemy of) joining others with Him.

Summary: There is only Allah. It is blasphemy to say there is a Godhead.

The Bible is clear that there IS a Godhead. Once again the Qur'an is confirming that Allah is NOT God. Let's summarize two critical points we have learned. First:

1. The Bible says Jesus is the Son of God.

2. The Qur'an says Jesus is NOT the son of Allah.

3. Therefore Allah cannot be God.

Second:

1. The Bible shows that Christ is God.

2. The Qur'an says it is blasphemy to say Christ is Allah.

3. Therefore Allah cannot be God.

What more evidence do we need? Allah, the moon god of Arabia is not God.

If, by believing and practicing the gospel of Jesus Christ, one becomes the enemy of Allah, who is this Allah that is so offended by the gospel of Christ?

… If by "hearing Him" (Jesus) we offend someone

named Allah, don't we have good reasons to research
the identity of this Allah?[9]

WHAT CAN I DO?

• Pray and do your part to reach Muslims for Christ.

• Don't be afraid to speak to a Muslim about Christ. Many
Muslims are searching. They have an unbelievably angry
god, and their religion leaves them no way to be forgiven.
Be willing to take a chance: say something!

• Pass out *Allah Had No Son* and other tracts regarding
the truth about Islam.

> * Pass them out to the precious Muslims.

> * Pass them out to fellow Christians. The more
> they know, the more they can do, too!

• Support efforts to bring God's word to the Muslims, in
unpolluted Bibles that do not use the pagan name "Allah"
instead of God.

• Read up on the truth about Islam. Here are some books
available from Chick Publications that will inform you:

> • *Christ, Muhammad and I*
> • *Who Is This Allah?*
> • *Anatomy of the Qur'an*
> • *The Islamic Invasion*

---

9) ***Who Is This Allah?*** by G.J.O. Moshay (2008), pp. 54-55. Available
from Chick Publications.

WHICH ONE IS THE LIVING GOD?

Who changed the truth of God into a lie, and worshipped and served the creature more than the Creator, who is blessed for ever. Amen.

Romans 1:25

There is a cancer that affects the lives of families worldwide. Nobody wants to talk about it. But it leads to the destruction of the children. This is a warning everybody needs to read.

Get off my back, Linda! I've been out all day looking for a job, and I'm tired.

There just isn't anything to be found.

We've been through all this before. *Quit throwing it in my face!*

You girls **turn** off that TV and get your work done!

I want the floors mopped and the dishes done.

Aw, Mom!

There's leftovers in the refrigerator for you to heat up for your dad.

Make sure you clean up after yourselves. I *don't* want to find a mess when I get home.

I've got to go to the store. I'll be back in about an hour.

I expect dinner to be ready when I get home.

I've got to get out of here before I go **nuts!** I need a drink.

Hey, that might be a good idea. There's nothing on TV tonight.

GRAND OPENING
FREE RENTAL
with Purchase of any Adult Film

ADULT FILMS

OPEN

LATER, AT HOME

KNOCK KNOCK

(Gasp)... I'd better hide this. Linda will **kill** me if she finds I've spent more money on these porno flicks.

Oh, uh, hi there, Charlie.

You look a little *guilty*, old buddy. Whatcha been up to?

Oh, nothing, Charlie. I'm just watching a movie.

Good. I'll come in and join you.

Some of this stuff is pretty kinky, Henry... but not as wild as what my **daughter** told me.

You know, Henry, I **know** about your "little secret."

What secret?

I know what's going on with Lisa. That's pretty juicy gossip.

I'll keep quiet, old buddy, *if* we can share and share alike.

TWO MONTHS LATER

Mr. Walker, Lisa's tests show that it **isn't** just a rash.

Then what is it?

Herpes Simplex Type II. I think we **need** to talk.

I'll go to **prison!** What'll I do? Everybody's going to know what I've done. I can't face being locked up. I'm going to **kill** myself.

Henry, I'm not only your doctor. I'm also your friend.

I **know** what's been going on. Lisa told me the whole ugly story about you and the neighbor when I made the tests.

SHE LIED!

No, Henry, I've examined Lisa, and I **know** she's telling the truth. She was sexually abused.

What a mess!

Yes, it's true. Oh, *God,* how did this ever happen?

Only *God* can help you, Henry.

I never *meant* for this to happen! It all started when my marriage began falling apart. I lost my job, and my wife had to go to work.

I started drinking and my wife started pulling away from me. Linda doesn't have any **respect** for me any more.

I can't even make a decent friend. I guess I'm a **total failure!**

Henry, **God** sees it all. He sees what's happening all over the world. **Every** home and every secret is open to His eyes. The Bible tells us that nothing is hidden.*

Don't you *get* it? I could go to **prison** for this!

*See Hebrews 4:13

True, but you're headed for a **far** worse place than that, Henry.

How can you **say** a thing like that? I was always a *good person* until **this** happened.

Now I feel like a "Dr. Jekyll and Mr. Hyde" —like a creature of the night, but *basically,* I'm *good.*

Henry, men love darkness because their deeds are *evil.**

The Bible tells us no man is good.** "All have sinned and come short of the glory of God."****

*See John 3:19 **Romans 3:10 ***Romans 3:23

Okay, so I'm going to hell. *So what?* I've been told it's not so bad. I'll have **lots** of company. All my friends will be there. Haw, Haw!

You *don't* know what you're talking about, Henry.

You **bought** the lie that hell is going to be one big party.

In reality, hell is going to be a **never-ending nightmare**, a place of screams and utter torment.

It's more horrible than you can imagine.

You'll be completely aware of the torment surrounding you, in total darkness and absolutely **alone,** without hope.

Henry, Jesus spoke more about hell than anyone else because He wanted us to know that it is a very **real** place.

Why would God *want* us to go to hell?

He doesn't!

God is "...not willing that any should perish, but that all should come to repentance."*

*II Peter 3:9b

It looks like there's **no hope** for me.

First you tell me I'm going to **hell**.

Then you say that God **doesn't** want me there.

What am I supposed to *believe?*

God did something very **special** —He made a way for you to be with Him in heaven. But the choice is up to you.

You can either **take** it or **leave** it.

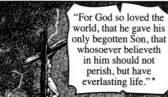

Jesus came to this world to die for you on the cross. He shed His **precious blood** to pay the *terrible price* for your sins.

"For God so loved the world, that he gave his only begotten Son, that whosoever believeth in him should not perish, but have everlasting life." *

*John 3:16

In other words, **He** took the punishment that *you* deserved.

That's God's love gift to you. *IF* you accept Jesus as your Saviour, He will set you free.

"If the Son therefore shall make you free, ye shall be free indeed." John 8:36

Pornography has turned you into a sexual predator and **ruined** your family. You've destroyed Lisa's innocence and given her an incurable S.T.D.*

You're going to **prison**, and at death into the **lake of fire**. *Only Jesus* can save your rotten soul.

*Sexually Transmitted Disease

Jesus said, "I am the way, the truth, and the life: no man cometh unto the father, but by me." John 14:6

You're **right,** Doctor. I've tried to change but it's gotten **worse.** I'm ready to try Jesus. But is He able to help me?

If I accept Jesus as my Saviour, will it last, or will I **still** have these problems?

Jesus said He will **not** allow Satan to tempt us beyond what we are able to bear.*

Jesus **knows** what you're going through. The Bible says Jesus was tempted in *all* things like we are, but without sin.** He understands.

*See 1 Corinthians 10:13   **See Hebrews 4:15

THEY PRAY, AND MOMENTS LATER

Doctor, I'm *so sorry* for what I've done. I'm so *ashamed.* I don't want to go to **hell!**

Will Jesus forgive someone as rotten as me?

Yes, Henry, *IF* you repent.* Let's pray.

*Jesus said, "Except ye repent, ye shall all likewise perish." Luke 13:3

I feel different, Doctor. *I feel clean.*

God has forgiven a *horrible* wretch like me.

Thank You, Lord! You're such a merciful and wonderful God to clean me up. *I'm so grateful!*

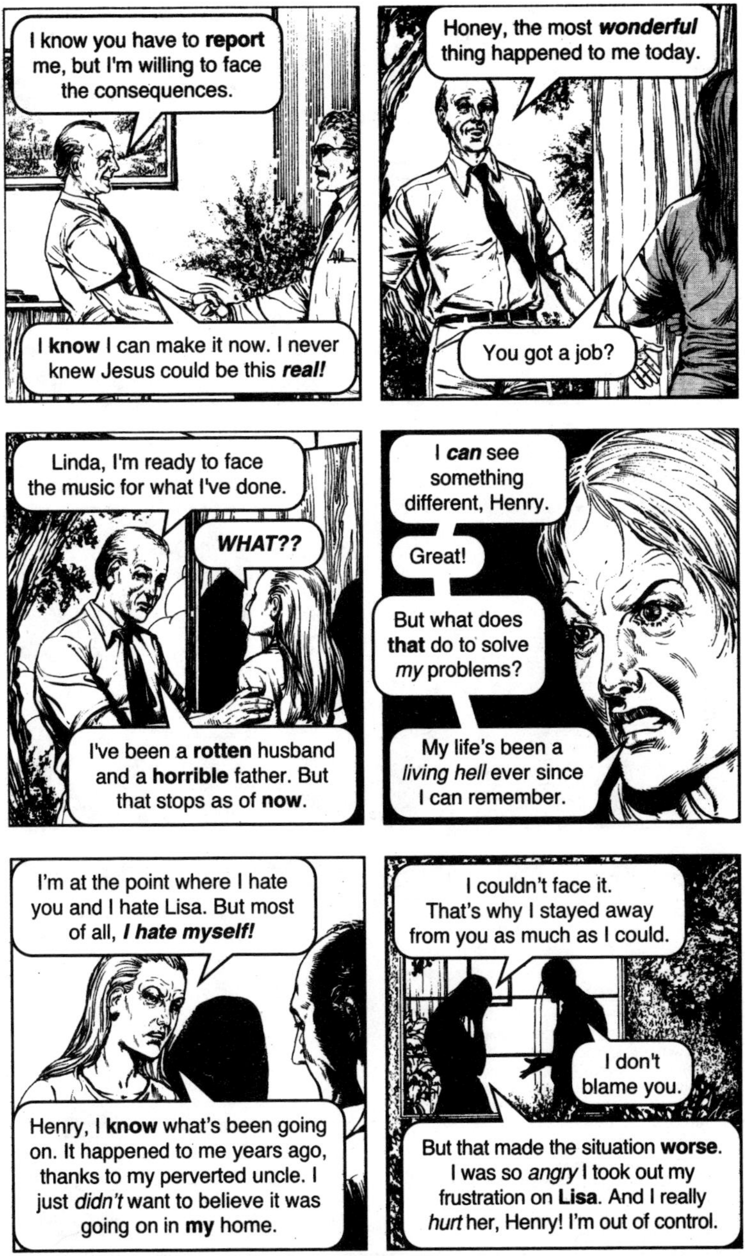
I know you have to **report** me, but I'm willing to face the consequences.
I **know** I can make it now. I never knew Jesus could be this ***real!***
Honey, the most ***wonderful*** thing happened to me today.
You got a job?
Linda, I'm ready to face the music for what I've done.
WHAT??
I've been a **rotten** husband and a **horrible** father. But that stops as of **now**.
I ***can*** see something different, Henry.
Great!
But what does **that** do to solve *my* problems?
My life's been a *living hell* ever since I can remember.
I'm at the point where I hate you and I hate Lisa. But most of all, ***I hate myself!***
Henry, I **know** what's been going on. It happened to me years ago, thanks to my perverted uncle. I just *didn't* want to believe it was going on in **my** home.
I couldn't face it. That's why I stayed away from you as much as I could.
I don't blame you.
But that made the situation **worse**. I was so *angry* I took out my frustration on **Lisa**. And I really *hurt* her, Henry! I'm out of control.

THE BIBLE SAYS THERE'S ONLY ONE WAY TO HEAVEN!

Jesus said, "I am the way, the truth, and the life: no man cometh unto the Father, but by me." John 14:6

NOBODY ELSE CAN SAVE YOU. TRUST JESUS TODAY!

"That if thou shalt confess with thy mouth the Lord Jesus, and shalt believe in thine heart that God hath raised him from the dead, thou shalt be saved." Rom. 10:9

1. Admit you are a sinner. See Romans 3:10
2. Be willing to turn from sin (repent). See Acts 17:30
3. Believe that Jesus Christ died for you, was buried and rose from the dead. See Rom. 10:9-10
4. Through prayer, invite Jesus into your life to become your personal Saviour. See Rom. 10:13

WHAT TO PRAY

Dear God, I am a sinner and need forgiveness. I believe that Jesus Christ shed His **precious blood** and died for my sin. I am willing to turn from sin. I now invite Christ to come into my heart and life as my personal Saviour.

If you trusted Jesus as your Saviour, you have just begun a wonderful new life with Him. Now:

1. Read your Bible every day to get to know Jesus Christ better.
2. Talk to God in prayer every day.
3. Be baptized, worship, fellowship, and serve with other Christians in a church where Christ is preached and the Bible is the final authority.
4. Tell others about Jesus Christ.

Here's help to grow as a new Christian! Read **The Next Step**, available at Christian bookstores or from Chick Publications.

"Pornography triggers sexual perversion"
—JTC

LISA

JTC There's a real sinister thing going on across the world. It seems that, in one generation after another, where parents have molested their children, they grow up, marry and themselves become molesters.

Some wives try to hold their families together, yet they know this evil thing is going on in the darkness of the night. It's a dreadful situation.

We did *Lisa* in hopes that people who are used and abused like this, when they come to Christ, they will be able to stop this satanic influence that pours from one generation to another. I want them to say, "This is enough! I'm putting the brakes on it. It's not going to happen again. I want my children to be protected and happy. I will *never* let this happen in my home. ***Never again!***"

That's the basis of *Lisa,* because this is a frequent problem, even in households that put on the image of being wonderful families. But it's more likely to hit when the wife remarries and the child is not his. When they drink, and watch filthy TV channels, and the man gets emotionally excited and creeps into the child's bedroom…. the child has no protection. This is a great evil that we tried to stop with *Lisa*, to show that trusting Jesus is the only way out.

DWD Read this heartbreaking story and the documentation that goes with it, because it is far more widespread than anyone cares to admit. The tract has a disturbing ending. You see how *little* this girl is, how *young* she is…

JTC Age has nothing to do with it; they can be much tinier than "Lisa." Children have been abused almost from birth in some cases. It's a horror out there. But at least we try our best and do what we can to alert people. This book could give children the awareness that such a thing happens and they can sound the alarm—

DWD —And that it's *wrong*….

JTC Yes! V*ery* wrong!

DWD There are even people who think such things are *natural*, right?

JTC That's right. We know a case with a girl who was saved reading *Somebody Loves Me*. Her dad had passed her around —when she was **three months old!** He was a police officer from Australia, and he was handing her to his friends.

He told people who molested her as she grew up (he was *selling her* as a prostitute, as a *young child)*, "You can beat her, do whatever you want, but don't cut her face." And they would put her in a cheap cubicle with paper-thin walls and he'd say, "Don't worry; she won't make a sound."

This girl was rescued from her life of abuse and got saved.

But she had thought, "Well, doesn't **everybody** have somebody like that in their family to help make money and keep the family going?" It's **insanity!** But thankfully she got saved.

DWD After the December 2004 tsunami hit Thailand, we learned that one of the "businesses" that it "disrupted" was where the Europeans would come in and parents would sell their children for unnatural acts with these tourists as a "vacation package."

Hopefully this story will help people become more aware of this horrible epidemic.

JTC That's the reason we did this book. Somebody has to blow the cover on this, and it should be the Christians who stand up for the children. It is the **molesters** who should have the fear of God in them —not the poor molested children.

HOW COULD THIS HAPPEN...
AND WHAT CAN WE DO ABOUT IT?

Child abuse. It's so predictable… and so preventable.

How could this be happening?

We all recoil in horror when we hear of another child who is molested by a selfish and uncontrolled adult predator. We weep for the little boy or girl. We hurt for them, knowing they will grow up with these scars, and that it will affect every relationship they have for the rest of their lives.

And the physical effects —some children are given incurable STDs by these monsters! What child deserves that? The molester behaves in a depraved and sick manner, ignoring the consequences of his or her actions. And it is the children who suffer.

It is like these molesters are in a completely different world from the rest of us. But what causes this horrible state of mind? One of the main causes is pornography.

People claim reading and viewing pornography is a "victimless crime." But look where it can lead.

Judith Reisman carefully researched and wrote a book on this subject: *"Soft Porn" Plays Hardball.*[1] In it she shows how *Playboy, Penthouse, Hustler* and others are written and drawn (they have comics in them, too) taking away the value from children and using them as actual "sex objects" to be used and abused by adults. Here is just one example from *Hustler:*

• Dwaine Tinsley, creator of the comic "Chester the Molester," wrote 145 child abuse cartoons during the 1980s "with child abuse and rape as the overriding theme." In an interview he claimed:

> I don't think I was legitimizing child molesting. Chester was just a goofy kinda guy.[2]

---

1) *"Soft Porn" Plays Hardball: Its Tragic Effects on Women, Children & the Family,* by Judith A. Reisman, Ph.D. (Lafayette, Louisiana: Huntington House Publishers, 1991).
2) Interview for the movie *Rate It X* (1988).

Tinsley was convicted in May 1989 of multiple counts of child molestation against his own daughter, drugging her, putting her on birth control at age 13, and violently sexually abusing her until she turned 18. According to Reisman, by that time she was "a suicidal drug addict."[3]

PORNOGRAPHY IS *NOT* A "VICTIMLESS CRIME"

In 1984 the US Senate held hearings on the "Effect of Pornography on Women and Children." John B. Rabun Jr., Chief Operating Officer of the National Center for Missing and Exploited Children told the senate that after investigating 1,400 cases of suspected child exploitation:

> …all —that is, 100% of the arrested pedophiles, child pornographers, pimps, what have you —all of these, in effect, child molesters, had in their possession at the time of arrest, adult pornography ranging from what is in the literature typically referred to as soft pornography such as *Playboy*, on up to harder, such as *Hustler*….[4]

Jesus stated it plainly: all lustful thoughts begin in the heart:

> But I say unto you, That whosoever **looketh on a woman to lust after her** hath committed adultery with her already in his heart.[5]

And:

---

3) *"Soft Porn" Plays Hardball* (1991), pp. 102-103.
4) *"Soft Porn" Plays Hardball* (1991), pp. 151-152.
5) Matthew 5:28.

> **For from within, out of the heart of men, proceed**
> **evil thoughts, adulteries, fornications**, murders,
> thefts, covetousness, wickedness, deceit, lasciviousness, an evil eye, blasphemy, pride, foolishness: **All**
> **these evil things come from within, and defile**
> **the man.**[6]

What is reading or watching pornography, but "looking on a woman to lust after her"? Jesus said these things "come from within, and defile" the person. It is something that comes out of the heart, but it is enflamed by what the eyes see.

Pornography is just as big an evil as child abuse because one often leads to the other.

In this age of mass communications, it seems impossible that there would be a crime that is not splattered all over the Internet and the evening news. But there is. The awful reality is that child sexual abuse remains an extremely *under*reported crime.

At least **one million Americans** are victims of father-daughter incest, and 16,000 more cases happen each year, according to estimates by Dr. David Finkelhor.[7] But the numbers may be *much larger* when considering females born

---

6 Mark 7:21-23.

7) David Finkelhor, Ph.D., is a Social Science professor at the University of New Hampshire. He specializes in issues related to family violence and has investigated child abuse issues since 1977. He is the Director of the Crimes Against Children Resource Center and Co-Director of the Family Research Laboratory.

into minority and low-income households.[8] Two-thirds of all state prisoners serving time for rape or sexual assault in 1991 victimized children, three-fourths of them young girls.[9] According to the South Eastern Centre Against Sexual Assault (SECASA):[10]

> The overwhelming majority of children are assaulted in their own or the offender's home by a male they know and trust. In most cases the perpetrator is the father, stepfather, grandfather, brother, uncle or mother's *de facto*.[11]

There are also boys who are violated by their parents, but those numbers are hard to obtain, since many boys are taught that their abuse is a "learning experience"[12] that happens in every family. It's supposed to help them "learn their orientation" or "face life as an adult."

Where does it start? For countless people, it starts with pornography or being abused as children themselves. Then it spirals into ever-deeper levels of depravity. Once they cross the generational line, it is extremely difficult to come back. Then another generation of children is abused.

---

8) See Aphrodite Matsakis, *When the Bough Breaks* (Oakland, CA: New Harbinger Publications, 1998).

9) See Lawrence Greenfield, *Child Victimizers: Violent Offenders and Their Victims: Executive Summary.* (Washington DC: Bureau of Justice Statistics and the Office of Juvenile Justice and Delinquency Prevention, US Dept of Justice, 1996.)

10) SECASA is located in Australia, but their information is online at: www.secasa.com.au

11) *De facto* means current boyfriend or other kind of partner.

12) See the information on incest from The National Center for Victims of Crime at www.ncvc.org

These abused people *desperately* need to know that this is not what God wants. He loves them, and He died to pay the price to get them to heaven and He will *never* abuse them. He also paid the price to transform their lives here on earth while they are still alive, and turn something sinful and ugly that happened to them into something He can use for His glory.

Those who commit such heinous acts need to know that they have sinned against God and those children. Only the shed blood of Jesus Christ will pay for what they have done. They must turn to Christ or they will suffer everlasting torment. But even if they receive Jesus, they will have to face up to their crimes.

Child abuse is a serious, growing problem. But there is no known way to stop a child abuser from hurting children, unless he is completely reshaped by God from the inside out as a "new creature" (2 Cor. 5:17). Without a change of heart by the washing of the blood of Jesus, there will be many more abused children. But with Christ there is always hope, both for the abused and for the abuser. Somehow we must get the gospel to both, while there is still time.

PROTECT YOUR CHILDREN

• **Keep your kids away from porn.** But realize this: it's not only in "adult magazines." It's rampant on the Internet, it's blatant in movie after movie, and it's thrown in our faces even on TV and commercials!

• Educate your kids about its horrible effects.

• Teach your children what Jesus said about their thought life.

• Be aware of what your kids are doing! Check what websites they are going to—what they are watching on television—what music they are listening to—what they are doing when they are with their friends.

• Don't let them have internet access in places where they are alone and can't be monitored.

• Change your own actions and habits. Find out the content of movies before you watch them. Don't be afraid to turn off the television, return the video or leave the movie theater. Remember, you are the example of Jesus your children will look to most. They don't just copy what you say; even more they copy what you do. Set a good example.

• Most importantly, pray for your kids every day.

WHAT ABOUT YOU?

Recognize your own "trigger points." Know what sets off your own lusts and desires inside you. Everybody has them. Don't "steel yourself against temptation." FLEE IT!

> Flee also youthful lusts: but follow righteousness, faith, charity, peace, with them that call on the Lord out of a pure heart.[13]

---

13) 2 Timothy 2:22.

In the 1990s, the "hate crime" broke new ground. What you *believe* became a crime, instead of what you *did*. Will these new laws threaten our right to share the gospel with the lost?

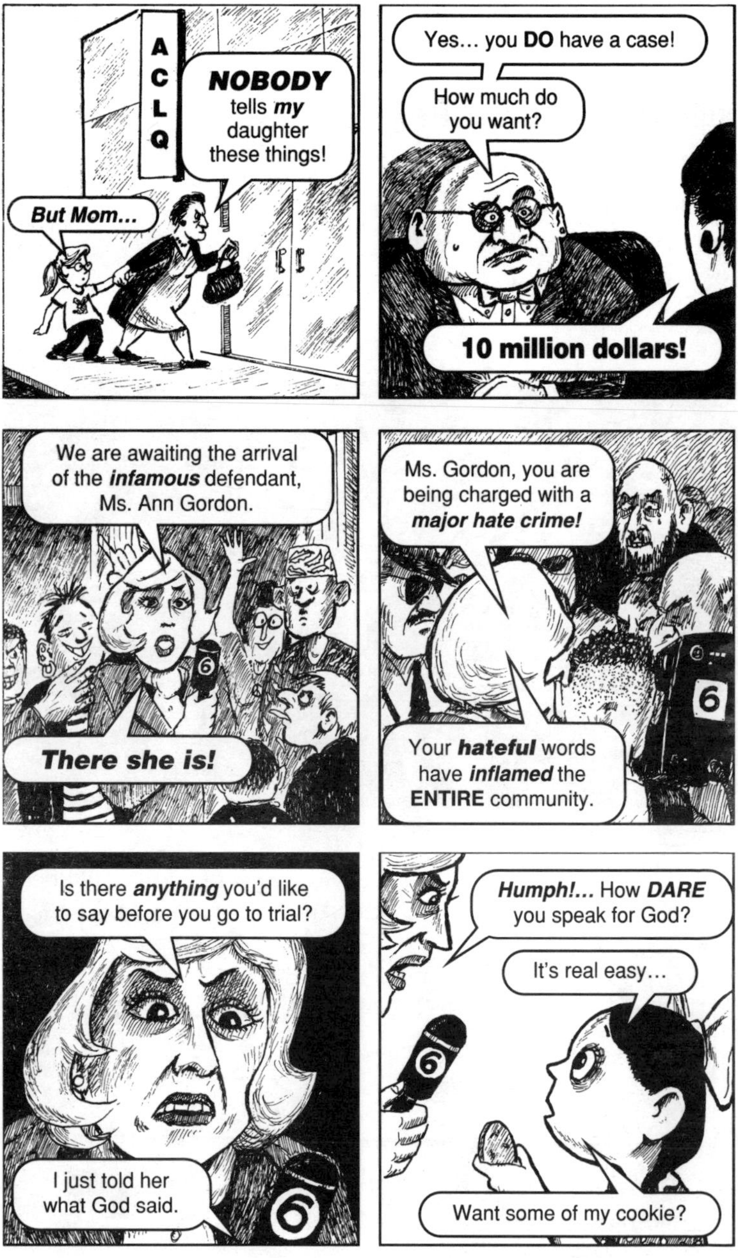
ACLQ
NOBODY tells my daughter these things!
But Mom...
Yes... you DO have a case!
How much do you want?
10 million dollars!
We are awaiting the arrival of the infamous defendant, Ms. Ann Gordon.
There she is!
Ms. Gordon, you are being charged with a major hate crime!
Your hateful words have inflamed the ENTIRE community.
Is there anything you'd like to say before you go to trial?
I just told her what God said.
Humph!... How DARE you speak for God?
It's real easy...
Want some of my cookie?

Your honor, I will be calling *highly* respected clergymen...

From *four* major religions that have been offended.

I will show that the defendant violated Mrs. Baxter's civil and religious rights...

And purposely *brainwashed* her child.

Your honor, I submit Exhibit A. This piece of *hate literature* was handed to my client's daughter.

Jesus said...
"I am the way, the truth, and the life: no man cometh unto the Father, but by me."
John 14:6

That's a LIE!

Hateful!

ORDER in the court!

There are **MANY** ways to heaven.

I call Bishop Danny O'Tool... a respected **man of God,** and the author of 17 *bestselling* books.

Proceed, Counselor.

There is **NO** salvation outside the church of Rome.* By *what* authority can this girl cause such division...

Among those of us who are *sacred?*

*1994 Catechism of the Catholic Church. Pg. 215. #816

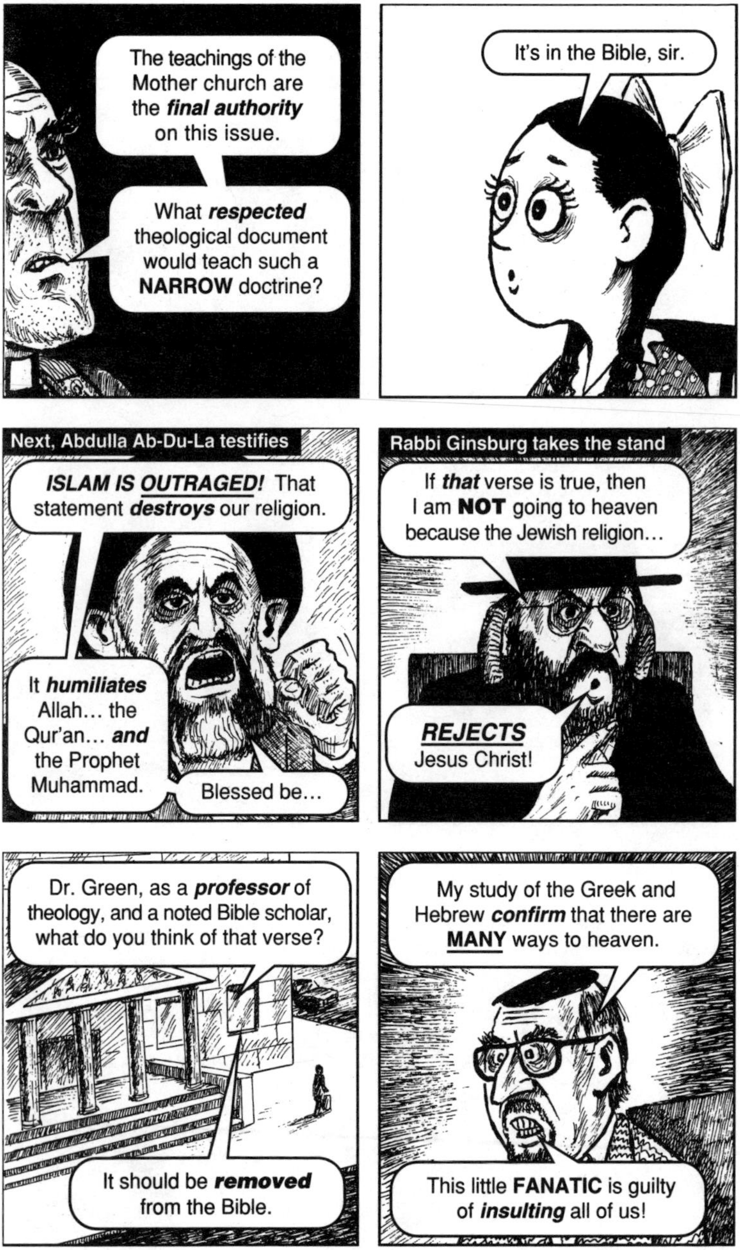
The teachings of the Mother church are the *final authority* on this issue.
What *respected* theological document would teach such a **NARROW** doctrine?
It's in the Bible, sir.
Next, Abdulla Ab-Du-La testifies
ISLAM IS OUTRAGED! That statement *destroys* our religion.
It *humiliates* Allah... the Qur'an... *and* the Prophet Muhammad.
Blessed be...
Rabbi Ginsburg takes the stand
If *that* verse is true, then I am **NOT** going to heaven because the Jewish religion...
REJECTS Jesus Christ!
Dr. Green, as a *professor* of theology, and a noted Bible scholar, what do you think of that verse?
It should be *removed* from the Bible.
My study of the Greek and Hebrew *confirm* that there are **MANY** ways to heaven.
This little **FANATIC** is guilty of *insulting* all of us!

Ms. Gordon, what did you say to Debbie Baxter?

I told Debbie that Jesus was the *only* way she could get to heaven.

He's the *ONLY* way for you, too, judge.

Just answer the questions, young lady.

The emotional stress of this **HATEFUL** attack has almost caused me to have a breakdown.

Lastly, your Honor, I call Debbie Baxter to the stand.

I'm counting on you, baby.

When I told Mama what Annie said, she *dragged* me to the lawyer.

I didn't get to tell her the **BEST** part.

PLEASE tell the court what else took place.

When Annie told me I should ask Jesus into my heart, *I did!*

Now I **love** God and *everybody*...

And *Jesus* is my way to heaven... because Jesus *DOESN'T LIE!*

$10,000,000

Case dismissed!

Yike!

Many years later, the mother and four accusers have passed into eternity.

Mom

Bishop O'Tool

Abdulla Ab-Du-La

Rabbi Ginsburg

The Rev. Dr. Green

Then a *STARTLING* event occurs.

All five rise from their graves.*

*John 5:28-29

Ooops! They thought the trial was all over... *but it wasn't!*

A much higher court takes over.

The One who will judge nations and every man, woman and child who ever lived now demands an account for their actions.

"He that hath the Son (Jesus) hath life; and he that hath not the Son of God hath not life." 1 John 5:12

"Neither is there salvation in any other: for there is none other name under heaven given among men, whereby we must be saved." Acts 4:12

*1 Pet. 1:18-19

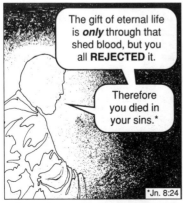

*Jn. 8:24

*Mt. 25:41

Satan does **NOT** want you to believe the gospel, so he and his followers call it **"Hate Literature."**

"For they that are such serve not our Lord Jesus Christ, but their own belly; and by good words and fair speeches deceive the hearts of the simple." Rom. 16:18

No matter what *anybody* tells you...*

Jesus is the *ONLY* way to heaven.

If **YOU** want to go there, do what it says on the next page.

*2 Cor. 11:3

THE BIBLE SAYS THERE'S ONLY ONE WAY TO HEAVEN!

Jesus said, "I am the way, the truth, and the life: no man cometh unto the Father, but by me." John 14:6

NOBODY ELSE CAN SAVE YOU. TRUST JESUS TODAY!

"That if thou shalt confess with thy mouth the Lord Jesus, and shalt believe in thine heart that God hath raised him from the dead, thou shalt be saved." Rom. 10:9

1. Admit you are a sinner. See Romans 3:10
2. Be willing to turn from sin (repent). See Acts 17:30
3. Believe that Jesus Christ died for you, was buried and rose from the dead. See Rom. 10:9-10
4. Through prayer, invite Jesus into your life to become your personal Saviour. See Rom. 10:13

WHAT TO PRAY

Dear God, I am a sinner and need forgiveness. I believe that Jesus Christ shed His **precious blood** and died for my sin. I am willing to turn from sin. I now invite Christ to come into my heart and life as my personal Saviour.

If you trusted Jesus as your Saviour, you have just begun a wonderful new life with Him. Now:

1. Read your Bible every day to get to know Jesus Christ better.
2. Talk to God in prayer every day.
3. Be baptized, worship, fellowship, and serve with other Christians in a church where Christ is preached and the Bible is the final authority.
4. Tell others about Jesus Christ.

Here's help to grow as a new Christian! Read **The Next Step**, available at Christian bookstores or from Chick Publications.

They were on the offensive, and the Christians were backpedaling. —JTC

THE TRIAL

JTC *The Trial* was written when I saw the Civil Rights Movement pushing "hate crimes" legislation, and I saw the writing on the wall. The concept of "free speech" becoming a "hate crime" could put a chill on the willingness of pastors to speak against homosexuality from their pulpits. Think of how "offensive" Jesus was, and what they did to Him when He said "I am THE way."

This impacts Muslims, Catholics, Mormons —every group you can think of. They're pushing their own agenda. But Jesus sidesteps them *completely* when He says, "I am the way, the truth, and the life: no man cometh unto the Father, but by me."[1] These simple words of Jesus tear out the foundations for their phony religions.

DWD You have talked about how, when you wrote this, you thought back to when a famous speaker started talking against homosexuality and she got denounced as a hateful person. What happened?

JTC We were at a CBA (Christian Booksellers Association)

---

1) See John 14:6.

convention in the 1970s. Anita Bryant, a very beautiful woman who almost won Miss America,[2] was the spokesperson for Florida Orange Juice. She had made a stand against homosexuality. She was the first entertainer who actually had the courage to say something. This became a turning point in this whole big movement. The entertainment people all turned against her. And (believe it or not) it was pretty much led by the snide and ugly comments made by Bob Hope.

So *everybody* jumped on the bandwagon. And poor Anita took a beating. They dumped her from being the Florida Orange Juice Lady. [3]

And a group of homosexuals humiliated her at the CBA convention we were attending. In the evening she was going to sing. Just as the music began, the homosexual crowd upstairs started stomping their feet on the ceiling above us to completely disrupt the whole thing. She was embarrassed. It was odd back then to see these people finally coming out and making a major attack against *one* individual.

There was a gay demonstration outside. Some of the pastors came up to our little booth where we were displaying Chick tracts and literature. They cleaned out our supply of *Gay Blade* tracts, then ran out and started passing them through the homosexual crowd.

But I could see we were in trouble. They were on the offensive, and the Christians were backpedaling. Christians

---

2) She was Miss Oklahoma in 1958 and 2nd runner-up for Miss America in 1959.

3) Her contract was "allowed to lapse" when it was up in 1979.

were *pacifying* them, and nobody objected. I thought, *"Man, if we don't make a stand, we're dead meat out there."* So I prayed about it, knowing these laws were going to eventually be passed, and came up with *The Trial.*

DWD So they first accused Christians of "hate speech" in the 1970s, during the days of Anita Bryant. Then in the 1990s you saw the widespread results in our country.

JTC Yeah, I felt so sorry for Anita. And by the 1990s I knew they were going to hit the churches and everything else. I saw that once these "hate laws" started, they'd try to kill the gospel if they could.

DWD I notice you had Muslims in this tract.

JTC Yes, because they were on the offensive, as well. You know, it seems today that *everyone* is on the offensive. This spirit of fear and intimidation has swept over the land. People are fearful of lawsuits, hate laws, and imprisonment.

Jesus, the disciples, and the prophets all ended up before courts. And they took a *stand.* Thank God they did. It's time for **us** to take a stand. If we don't, in the future we may meet each other behind razor wire in a concentration camp.

I believe that Christians —born-again believers who make a stand for Christ—will become as vulnerable as the Jews of Nazi Germany. God's going to be with the Jews in the future. But unless the Lord comes (and I believe He will, with the rapture, to take us out before the end hits), we may have to face the world's hatred.

DWD So, when hate crimes legislation trumps free speech

rights in our country, there will be nobody to blame but us. The information *was here in this tract years ago.*

JTC "Judgment must begin at the house of God."[4] Unless God's people repent and God sends a revival, it will hit us.

◆   ◆   ◆

WHY PUBLIC BIBLE READING MAY SOON BE ILLEGAL

Worldwide, "hate crimes" are being used to justify taking away freedom of speech. Look at these recent examples:

• Is reading the Bible out loud "hate speech?"

In Sweden, 64-year-old Pastor Ake Green was sentenced to one month in prison for preaching and reading Bible verses against homosexuality *in his own church pulpit.* Sweden had added "sexual orientation" to its "hate crime" law. The government prosecutor said, "Collecting Bible [verses] on this topic, as he does, makes this hate speech."

The next year the charges were dismissed, but only after the entire case against him was broadcast on live television for all the world to see.[5]

---

4) See 1 Peter 4:17.

5) For more on this and other "hate crimes," visit www.repentamerica.com

• Is drawing a caricature of Muhammad "hate speech?"

Philippe Val, editor of the satirical French newspaper *Charlie Hebdo*, published some cartoons of Muhammad with the front-page headline, "Mohammed Overwhelmed by Extremists." It had a drawing of Muhammad with his hands covering his eyes, crying, "It's hard to be loved by idiots," and two other caricatures.

The Grand Mosque of Paris and the Union of Islamic organizations of France quickly sued, claiming he had "publicly abused a group because of their religion."[6]

That could have resulted in six months imprisonment and a fine of about $30,000. However, even the public prosecutor recommended acquittal, seeing nothing "injurious to the Muslim community" in the caricatures. It took a full year for Val to be acquitted, after a two-day trial and a number of letters from intellectuals written in his defense.

• Is calling homosexuality "abnormal and deviant" "hate speech?"

Dr. Laura Schlessinger, a radio talk show host, was rebuked by the Canadian Broadcast Standards Council for statements made during 11 programs. Her crime? She recommended counseling and therapy to people who *wanted* a way out of their homosexual urges.

The Council stated that homosexuals are "defined by an innate or unchangeable characteristic," and their sexual

---

6) See "Modern Blasphemy" in the *Wall Street Journal*, March 21, 2007, Vol. CCXLIX, No. 66, p. A19.

practices "are as much a part of their being as the color of one's skin or the gender, religion, age or ethnicity of an individual." Because of that, they claimed that Schlessinger's professional opinions amounted to an "abusively discriminatory comment" in the eyes of Canadian law.

Since then, all of Dr. Laura's remarks about homosexuality have been cut out of every Canadian broadcast.

WHAT ABOUT THE UNITED STATES?

I'm afraid it isn't much different in the U.S.:

• **Is carrying signs and singing hymns a "hate crime?"**

As you learned in Chapter One, October 11th is now known as "Coming Out Day." People are encouraged to "come out" and admit they are gay, lesbian, bisexual or transgender.[7]

During the Philadelphia, Pennsylvania "Outfest" on October 11, 2004, a number of Christians walked into the fray, singing hymns and carrying signs calling for repentance.

A pro-gay group called "The Pink Angels" surrounded them and used large cut-outs of angels to keep them from moving. Police responded, and arrested —*the Christians!* The perpetrators who spent the night in jail ranged from a 17-year-old girl to a 72-year-old grandmother.

They were charged with three felonies and five "hate crimes" misdemeanors: riot, criminal conspiracy, possession of instruments of crime [which: their signs, or their voices?], reckless endangerment of another person, ethnic

---

7) These four are now grouped together, and known as "GLBT." Note the sign on the parade float at the beginning of the Chick tract, *Sin City.*

intimidation, failure to disperse, disorderly conduct [must be all that "disorderly" walking and singing] and obstructing highways.

The total charges would have added up to 47 *years* in jail. Finally in February 2005 a judge threw out all the charges, finding "no basis whatsoever for *any* of them." Can you imagine what would have happened if this judge had been a gay rights activist? And do you think 47 years is a *just* sentence for the "horrible, hateful crime" of carrying signs and singing hymns?

• Is it "*not* hate" when it's directed against Christians?

On June 14, 2005, a Christian group known as Repent America came to peaceably protest Philadelphia's "Gay Pride" parade. According to Repent America, this "city-funded event included simulated sex acts on one of the floats" and "partially dressed women bending over and being spanked by hands, whips and objects."

But the gay activists were alerted to the Christians' arrival. Philadelphia Anti-Racist Action called on people to block the Christians. Supporters gathered at the "Queers Bash Back" and "No Human Liberation without Queer Liberation" banners, then donned handkerchief masks and "surrounded, obstructed and continually harassed" the Christian protesters.

The **police**, informed of the lewd behavior and the gay supporters' obstruction of the Christians quickly **jumped into action** and did… *absolutely nothing*. Evidently, **hate directed against Christians is no crime**.

What is it about Pennsylvania that brought about these two abuses of justice? In 2002 the state added "actual or perceived sexual orientation" and "gender or gender identity" (what gender a person *thinks* or *feels* he or she is) to their "ethnic intimidation hate crimes" law. Christians warned people that this would lead to the persecution of Bible-believers, but as too often happens, no one listened till it was too late.

Lately legislators have continually tried to slip "hate crimes" legislation into bills on completely different subjects, like national defense. The president could quickly sign these into law, *and the public wouldn't even know until the ink dried.*

"HATE CRIME" LAWS ARE ABOUT SUPPRESSING YOUR FREE SPEECH

As Robert H. Knight, director of the Culture and Family Institute wrote:

> "Hate crime" laws pose a danger to civil liberties in three ways:
>
> - They pave the way for suppression of the freedoms of speech, association and religion.
> - They violate the concept of equal protection under the law.
> - They introduce the un-American concept of "thought crime," in which someone's actions are "more" illegal based on their thoughts or beliefs.[8]

In the USA, freedom of thought, speech, and writing has

---

8) See *'Hate Crime' Laws: An Assault on Freedom,* by Robert H. Knight (Sept 27, 2005). The Culture and Family Institute is an affiliate of Concerned Women for America, www.cwfa.org

formed the basis of our way of life. Many countries do not value these as we have. But these "hate crime" laws threaten to take those freedoms away. And if the courts take away *our* freedom to spread the gospel and tell people what the Bible says, what shall happen to the countries with *lesser* rights and freedoms than ours?

We are already ripe for God's judgment. Woe to us if we stop spreading the gospel for fear of some "hate crime" laws.

We are here for "such a time as this."

WHAT CAN I DO?

First and foremost, we must pray:

• Pray that God will withhold judgment on our country.

• Pray for the lost.

• Pray for our country and our leaders.

• Pray that Christians will see that this is a spiritual battle. The devil is hard at work trying to take away our right to share the gospel and give people the good news that can transform their lives and change their eternal destinies.

Secondly, we must speak out, telling everyone we can that speaking the truth as found in God's word is not hate.

We need to teach this to young people:

• Sunday School teachers can teach this to their classes.

• Youth workers can teach this to their youth groups.

• Boy Scout and Girl Scout leaders can teach this.

• Write letters to the editor and articles in other local periodicals.

• Start educating other people in your church. Start groups on the grass roots level to address this issue. To survive as a nation, we must have the right of free speech.

• Email elected officials.

• Pass out tracts to win people to Christ. Once the Spirit of God lives in them they will be much more likely to understand this issue.

For our nation to survive, Christians need to repent of their sins. "…except ye repent, ye shall all likewise perish" (Luke 13:3). Without repentance there will be no revival.

If we Christians lose our right to speak out on these vital subjects —we will have no one to blame but ourselves.

**…Nevertheless when the Son of man cometh,
shall he find faith on the earth?
Luke 18:8**

IN THE PAST	THINGS TO COME?
USE A GUN	**USE A BIBLE**

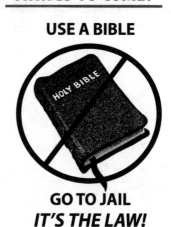

GO TO JAIL
IT'S THE LAW!

GO TO JAIL
IT'S THE LAW!

Should Christians play Dungeons & Dragons or other role-playing games? Many who call themselves Christians are deeply involved in the game, and vigorously defend it. But is this how Christians should spend their time? Take a closer look and see for yourself.

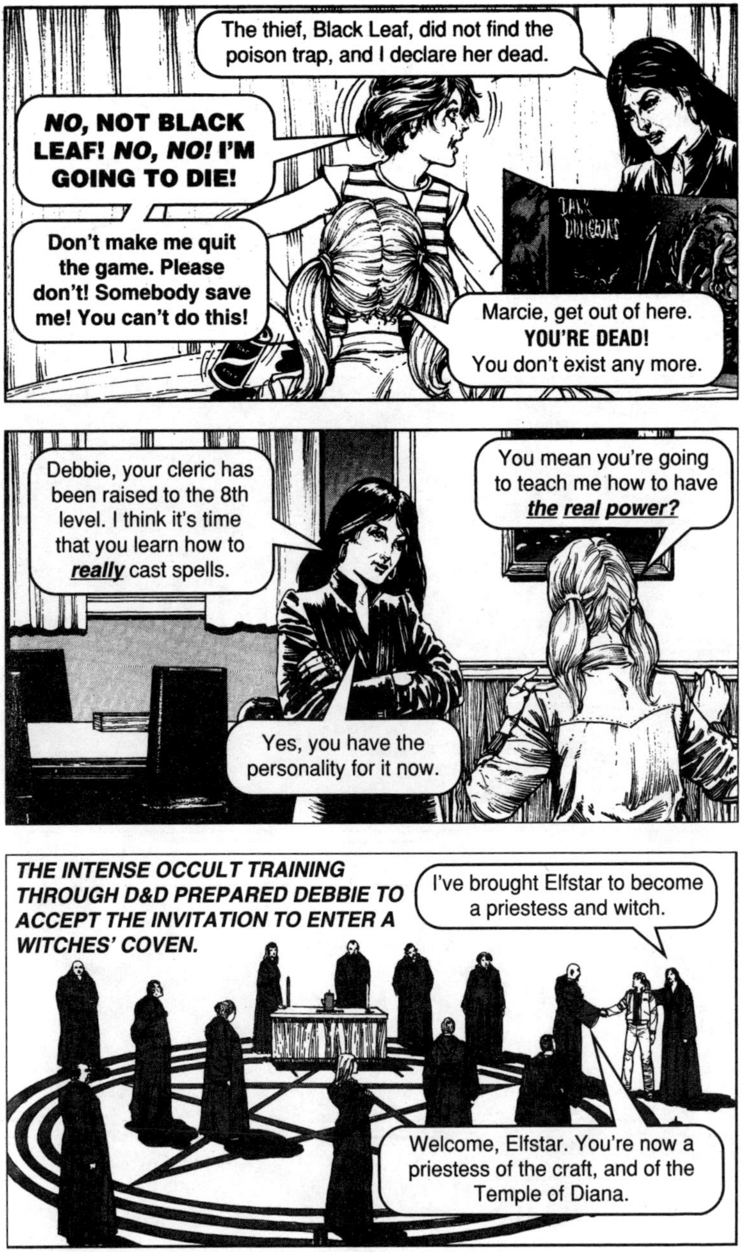
The thief, Black Leaf, did not find the poison trap, and I declare her dead.
***NO,* NOT BLACK LEAF! *NO, NO!* I'M GOING TO DIE!**
Don't make me quit the game. Please don't! Somebody save me! You can't do this!
Marcie, get out of here. **YOU'RE DEAD!** You don't exist any more.
Debbie, your cleric has been raised to the 8th level. I think it's time that you learn how to ***really*** cast spells.
You mean you're going to teach me how to have ***the real power?***
Yes, you have the personality for it now.
THE INTENSE OCCULT TRAINING THROUGH D&D PREPARED DEBBIE TO ACCEPT THE INVITATION TO ENTER A WITCHES' COVEN.
I've brought Elfstar to become a priestess and witch.
Welcome, Elfstar. You're now a priestess of the craft, and of the Temple of Diana.

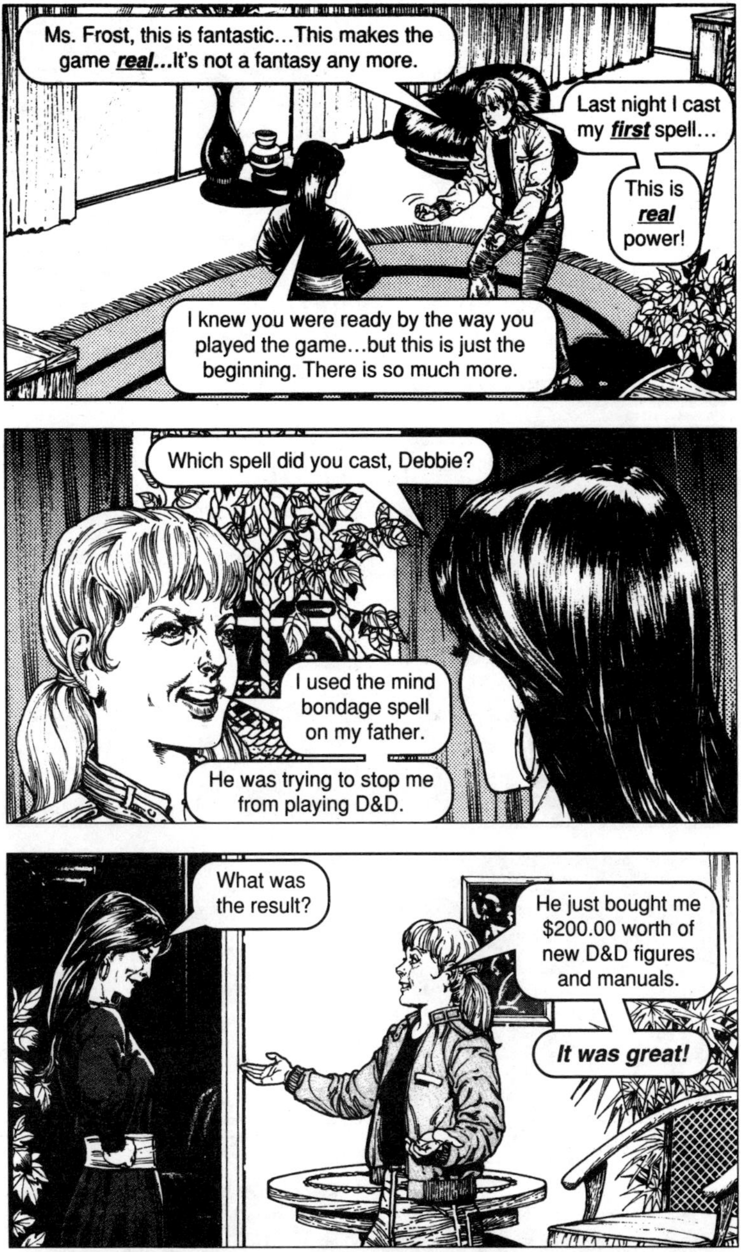
Ms. Frost, this is fantastic...This makes the game *real*...It's not a fantasy any more.
Last night I cast my *first* spell...
This is *real* power!
I knew you were ready by the way you played the game...but this is just the beginning. There is so much more.
Which spell did you cast, Debbie?
I used the mind bondage spell on my father.
He was trying to stop me from playing D&D.
What was the result?
He just bought me $200.00 worth of new D&D figures and manuals.
It was great!

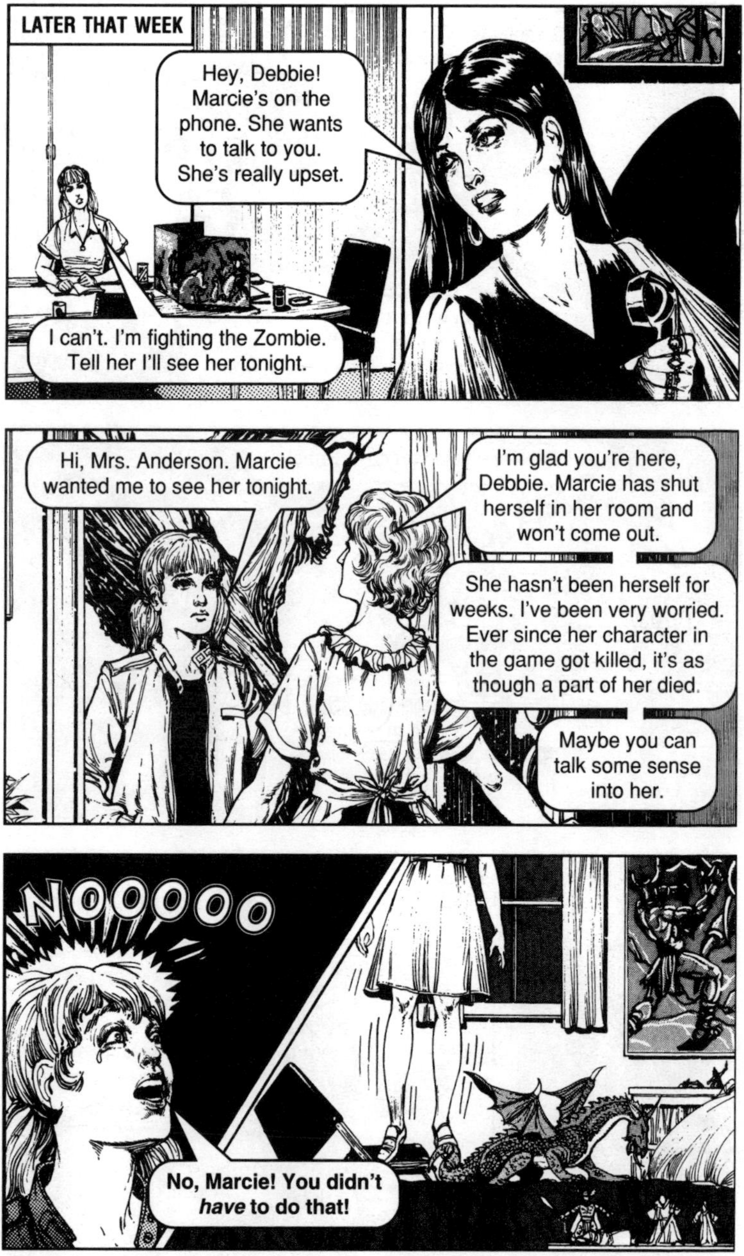
LATER THAT WEEK
Hey, Debbie! Marcie's on the phone. She wants to talk to you. She's really upset.
I can't. I'm fighting the Zombie. Tell her I'll see her tonight.
Hi, Mrs. Anderson. Marcie wanted me to see her tonight.
I'm glad you're here, Debbie. Marcie has shut herself in her room and won't come out.
She hasn't been herself for weeks. I've been very worried. Ever since her character in the game got killed, it's as though a part of her died.
Maybe you can talk some sense into her.
NOOOOO
No, Marcie! You didn't *have* to do that!

It's my fault Black Leaf died. I can't face life alone!
Marcie
Ms. Frost, I can't get Marcie out of my mind. How could she do something like this?
If I'd left the game, she'd be alive today.
Get your priorities straight, Debbie.
Your spiritual growth through the game is more important than some lousy loser's life.
It would have happened sooner or later. Her character was too weak.
But the law of our faith is that we can do anything we want as long as we harm no one. But now we have harmed Marcie.
What have I gotten myself into?

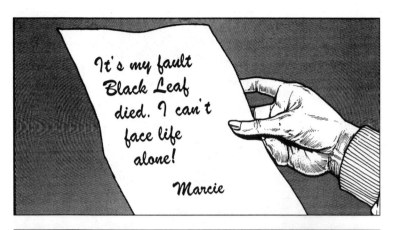

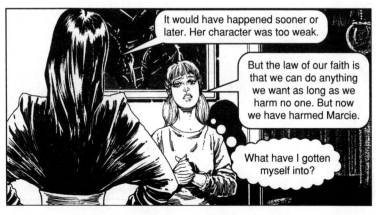

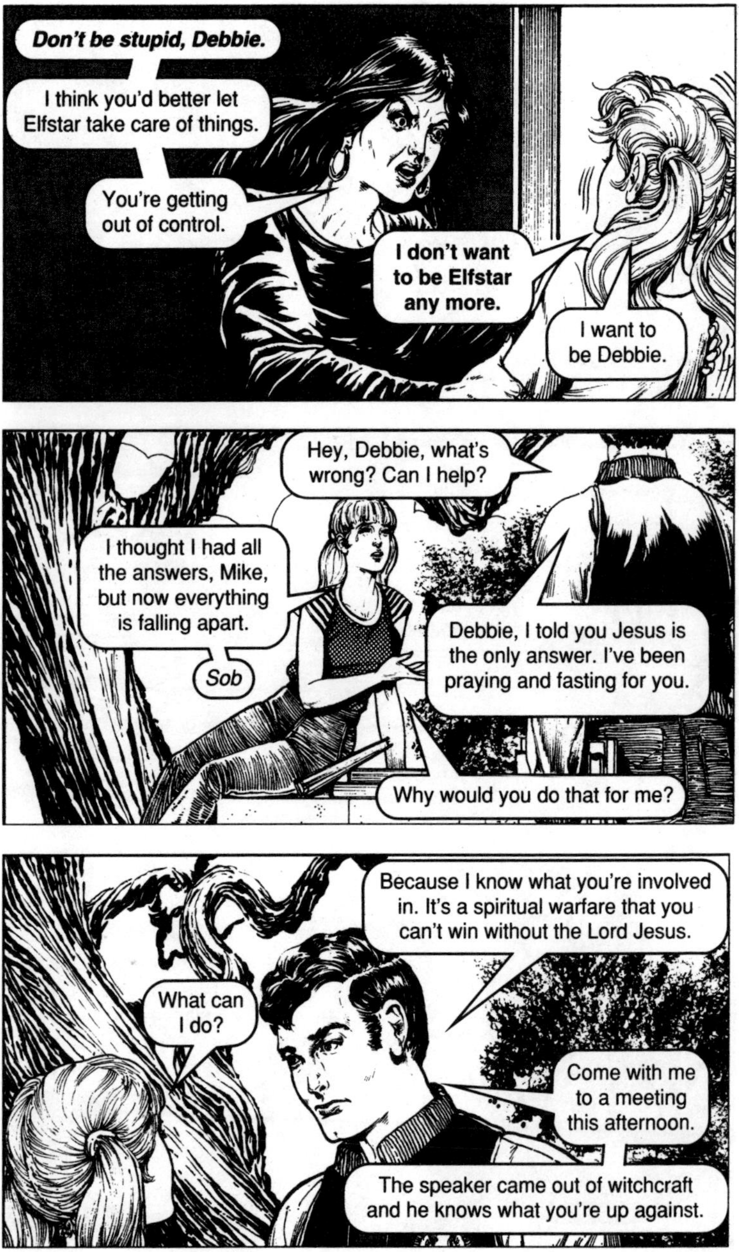
Don't be stupid, Debbie.
I think you'd better let Elfstar take care of things.
You're getting out of control.
I don't want to be Elfstar any more.
I want to be Debbie.
Hey, Debbie, what's wrong? Can I help?
I thought I had all the answers, Mike, but now everything is falling apart.
Sob
Debbie, I told you Jesus is the only answer. I've been praying and fasting for you.
Why would you do that for me?
Because I know what you're involved in. It's a spiritual warfare that you can't win without the Lord Jesus.
What can I do?
Come with me to a meeting this afternoon.
The speaker came out of witchcraft and he knows what you're up against.

THAT AFTERNOON

You, who are involved in the occult, think you have achieved power,

But you have been trapped in a dungeon of bondage.

The limited power you have been given is only bait to lure you to destruction.

But Jesus came that you might have life and that more abundantly.

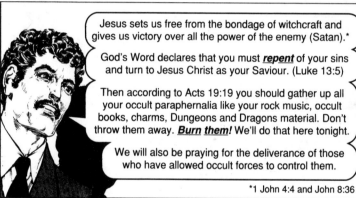

Jesus sets us free from the bondage of witchcraft and gives us victory over all the power of the enemy (Satan).*

God's Word declares that you must **_repent_** of your sins and turn to Jesus Christ as your Saviour. (Luke 13:5)

Then according to Acts 19:19 you should gather up all your occult paraphernalia like your rock music, occult books, charms, Dungeons and Dragons material. Don't throw them away. **_Burn them!_** We'll do that here tonight.

We will also be praying for the deliverance of those who have allowed occult forces to control them.

*1 John 4:4 and John 8:36

If you want Jesus as your Lord, come forward now.

Oh, God! I need help… My life's a mess. _Help me!_

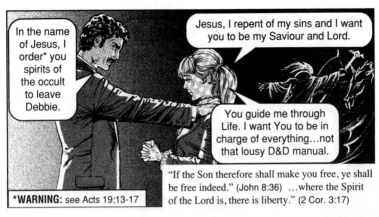

"There shall not be found among you anyone…that useth divination…or a witch,
…or a consulter with familiar spirits, or a wizard….For all that do these things are an
abomination unto the Lord."   Deut. 18:10-12

THE BIBLE SAYS THERE'S ONLY ONE WAY TO HEAVEN!

Jesus said, "I am the way, the truth, and the life: no man cometh unto the Father, but by me." John 14:6

NOBODY ELSE CAN SAVE YOU. TRUST JESUS TODAY!

"That if thou shalt confess with thy mouth the Lord
Jesus, and shalt believe in thine heart that God hath
raised him from the dead, thou shalt be saved." Rom. 10:9

1. Admit you are a sinner. See Romans 3:10
2. Be willing to turn from sin (repent). See Acts 17:30
3. Believe that Jesus Christ died for you, was
   buried and rose from the dead. See Rom. 10:9-10
4. Through prayer, invite Jesus into your life to
   become your personal Saviour. See Rom. 10:13

WHAT TO PRAY

Dear God, I am a sinner and need forgiveness. I
believe that Jesus Christ shed His **precious blood**
and died for my sin. I am willing to turn from sin. I
now invite Christ to come into my heart and life as
my personal Saviour.

If you trusted Jesus as your Saviour, you have just begun a wonderful new life with Him. Now:

1. Read your Bible every day to get to know
   Jesus Christ better.
2. Talk to God in prayer every day.
3. Be baptized, worship, fellowship, and serve
   with other Christians in a church where
   Christ is preached and the
   Bible is the final authority.
4. Tell others about
   Jesus Christ.

Here's help to grow as a new
Christian! Read **The Next Step**,
available at Christian bookstores
or from Chick Publications.

"Should Christians spend their waking hours plotting murder and mayhem?" —JTC

~~~ DARK DUNGEONS ~~~~~~~~~~~~~~~~~~~~~~~~~~~~

JTC The *Dark Dungeons* tract was a sleeper. When we published it I had no idea how it would play out. A friend who had come out of witchcraft warned me of the dangers of the game "Dungeons & Dragons."

In some RPGs (Role Playing Games) players can "become" their character. They dress like them, act like them and essentially "are" their character as they play the game.

In time, they begin to confuse their own identity with that of their character. So our story tells of someone who committed suicide because she lost out in the game. Her make-believe "world" came to an end.

The world of D&D was an underground world. Most Christians weren't aware of it, so they didn't know who to pass the tract to. They didn't *know* who played the game.

But the D&Ders knew of us. When the internet came along and we posted *Dark Dungeons* online, the gamers declared war on us. They stormed our website and pelted us with emails. They were offended —but they still got the gospel and will be without excuse on Judgment Day.

In fact, many click on through to other articles on our website that discuss D&D.

DWD And that hasn't changed much over the years.

JTC It has almost a cult following among the gamers. Many of the gaming sites still have links to the *Dark Dungeons* tract. Every day it is a very heavily-read page on the chick. com website.

DWD I still get emails from gamers. For fellow students, when I was in Bible college, it was like an addiction. There were about six guys who were once considered spiritual, godly people, good Christians, sons of missionaries, things like that, and they got involved in D&D. And it evolved into many hours a day playing the game. And boy, if you told them there was something wrong with it, they would scold your ears off.

JTC It becomes a compulsion.

DWD "Compulsion" is a good word for it. They were not only compelled to play, they were *fanatical* about playing. And guess what? If you are fanatical about playing D&D, you're **not** fanatical about the **gospel!** If you're so absorbed that you cannot get your mind out of the game, and you're always thinking about how to be Dungeon Master and how to get out of this pitfall and how to increase your strength points and how to break down your enemy's defenses, you are **not** thinking about the gospel.

JTC It's an absolute *diversion*. But it's more than that. Because the Bible says:

> …whatsoever things are **true**, whatsoever things
> are **honest**, whatsoever things are **just**, whatsoever
> things are **pure** …think on *these* things"[1]

The D&D gamers do not keep their minds dwelling on these things. They are thinking about death. They are thinking about murder. And the D&D books that teach them how to do it have information that was originally compiled from occultic books in order to provide *realism*.[2] This means they are **not** dwelling on the word of God.

DWD You told me the story about how you spoke to a young man in a video store who said he was a gamer. You asked him, "Can you 'see' the game yet?"

JTC Right, and he said, "Yes." "Seeing the game" was a code word for deep emotional involvement in the game, like Elfstar in the *Dark Dungeons* tract.

DWD Then should Christians play the game?

JTC That's simple. Let's just rephrase the question: Should a Christian spend most of his waking hours plotting murder, mayhem, how to cast spells and so on, in an effort to find ways to become the Dungeon Master?

Is this what the Lord has called us to do? These games are like pornography. They lure you into a different world, and there's almost no way to pull someone out of it. Only the power of the gospel can do that.

◆　　◆　　◆

---

1) Philippians 4:8.
2) See the interview with Bill Schnoebelen following.

BILL SCHNOEBELEN INTERVIEW

This interview with Bill Schnoebelen took place on April 14, 2008 regarding his connection to Dungeons & Dragons.

DWD How are you connected to the issue of D&D (Dungeons & Dragons)?

BILL Very early on in our time in Milwaukee we were setting up witch covens and such, and naturally, we had feelers out at our local colleges. We had some young students come in to get initiated into our coven, and several of them were Dungeons & Dragons players. Two of them were Dungeon Masters. They got to talking about it, and I played the game two or three times. I can hardly say I am an expert on that part of it.

But then one of them said, "Listen, I know some people who are working on these games down in Lake Geneva. (At that time we were in Milwaukee, and Lake Geneva was where TSR was, which at that time was the headquarters of Dungeons & Dragons). So they asked if they could arrange an interview between some game people from down there and my wife and I. So we met in their living room and they picked our brains about how to have more authentic magical spells in the game.

We tried to tell them, this is how you do ceremonial magic; this is how you cast spells; things like that. They spent a good three hours taking copious notes.

Now I cannot document that they went ahead and put everything we told them into the games, but I know there must have been some interest in that, because they wouldn't have spent all that time with us if they weren't interested in how to make their games more magically authentic.

DWD Did you have any connection with Gary Gygax (the original creator of Dungeons & Dragons)?

BILL I never met him but these were some of his employees. He was the founder of the company. He was the big genius behind Dungeons & Dragons. On his shoulders lay all of his offshoots, most of which are even worse than Dungeons & Dragons. But no, I never knew him.

To me the games were not all that interesting because it's a very engrossing, time-consuming thing, and I was more interested in being a *real* magician, rather than playing at being one.

THEY WANTED TO BECOME WITCHES
BECAUSE THEY PLAYED D&D

DWD So were these college people creators of D&D?

BILL No, they were just college people who were engrossed in the game. What is interesting is when I talked to them about all this and why they wanted to become witches. It was because they had been playing D&D and they saw we had posters up all around campus, advertising our group. So there is a direct correlation there, at least for those two or three guys, between being Dungeons & Dragons enthusiasts and being witches.

You see, Geneva is only 30-40 miles south of Milwaukee. And back then, the company making D&D wasn't some big enormous thing. It was a smaller, more intimate outfit. And there were these little networks of gamers all over the west coast of Lake Michigan, from Chicago up and down. And through that network they told somebody at TSR about us.

> "We know these people who are genuine sorcerers, they're real witches and magicians; and if they'd be willing to talk to you, would you like to meet them and know more about them?"

They did.

DWD How do people react to the articles you wrote on D&D at chick.com and your website?

Bill I get about 15-20 emails a week from people yelling at me about those articles. People often say they use D&D for soul-winning. You know, people will do *anything* to justify their sin. They'll find any little excuse they can. It is totally sad.

I'm astonished at how many Christians yell at me and curse at me and call me all manner of vile names, then tell me what a great Christian they are, while they play D&D every week.

D&D is not a game. It's a doorway to darkness.

♦   ♦   ♦

HOW TO CLIMB OUT OF THE DUNGEON

D&D and other RPGs are like coiled snakes. At any time they can strike, and you are disabled. You are pulled away from the light of Christ into something very dark.

Jesus said:

> Take heed therefore that the light which is in thee be not darkness.[3]

It is easy to say, "I'm just having fun, playing a game." But as Christians, we must answer to God for how we spend our time. God wrote through the apostle Paul:

> See then that ye walk circumspectly, *not as fools*, but as wise, ***redeeming the time***, because the days are evil.[4]

And:

> Walk in wisdom toward them that are without, ***redeeming the time***.[5]

People write Chick Publications, claiming to be church leaders, saying they "use" Dungeons & Dragons to win the lost. How? Be honest: what Christian principles are taught in this occult-based game? The Bible says:

> And ***have no fellowship with the unfruitful works of darkness***, but rather reprove them. For it is a shame even to speak of those things which are done of them in secret.[6]

---

3) Luke 11:35.
4) Ephesians 5:15-16.
5) Colossians 4:5.
6) Ephesians 5:11-12.

This is not just confined to a game like D&D. What do you spend your time watching? Is it sex and violence or blood and gore? How much time do you spend watching TV or movies?

Ouch. This hits a little closer to home, doesn't it?

In a 2006 survey,[7] George Barna found that "half of all American adults said that their life has been 'greatly transformed' by their religious faith."

How did this happen? Note this statistic:

> ... *people who read the Bible regularly were more than twice as likely as* those who do not to have undergone faith-based transformation, and **the same pattern** was true among *those who attend a church regularly* compared to those who do not.

Do you want God to transform your life? Spend your time wisely. Read your Bible and get with others in a Bible-believing church. As the Bible says:

> And let us consider one another to provoke unto love and to good works: Not forsaking the assembling of ourselves together, as the manner of some is; but exhorting one another: and so much the more, as ye see the day approaching.[8]

What should we think about, according to the scriptures?

> "...whatsoever things are **true**, whatsoever things are **honest**, whatsoever things are **just**, whatso-

---

7) "Half of Americans Say Faith Has 'Greatly Transformed' Their Life," by George Barna, *The Barna Update*, 6/6/06. www.barna.org
8) Hebrews 10:24-25.

ever things are **pure**, whatsoever things are **lovely**, whatsoever things are of **good report**; if there be any **virtue**, and if there be any **praise**, think on *these* things."[9]

If you are ensnared in the "unfruitful works of darkness," *come out!* Call on Jesus, confess your sin to Him, and ask for Him to forgive you for wasting the precious time He gave you on this earth.

Then spend all the extra time you suddenly have reading the Bible and fellowshipping with other Christians in a church where Christ is preached and the Bible is the final authority.

> **Wherefore come out from among them, and be ye separate, saith the Lord, and touch not the unclean thing; and I will receive you..."**[10]

The Lord gave us gospel tracts to reach our nation and our world. Let us no longer be silent:

> **"Go ye into all the world, and preach the gospel to every creature."** *Mark 16:15*

God bless you as you reach our world for Christ.

---

9) Philippians 4:8.
10) 2 Corinthians 6:17.

A Call to Action

"If religious literature is not widely circulated
Among the masses in this country,
I do not know what is going to become of us as a nation.
If truth be not diffused (promoted),
Error will be;
If God and His Word are not known and received,
The devil and his works will gain the ascendancy;
If the evangelical volume (the gospel)
Does not reach every hamlet,
The pages of a corrupt and licentious literature will;
If the power of the gospel is not felt
Throughout the length and breadth of the land,
Anarchy and misrule,
Degradation and misery,
Corruption and darkness,
Will reign without mitigation
Or end."

Daniel Webster, 1823

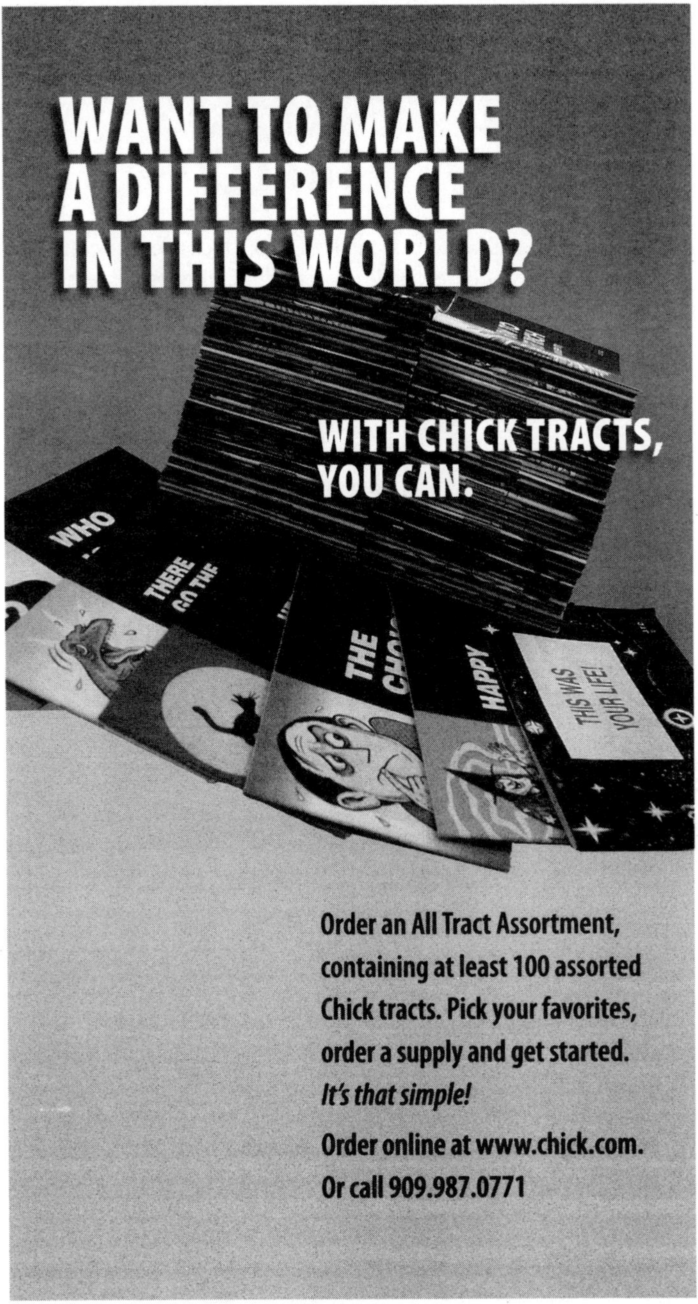
WANT TO MAKE A DIFFERENCE IN THIS WORLD?
WITH CHICK TRACTS, YOU CAN.
THIS WAS YOUR LIFE!
Order an All Tract Assortment, containing at least 100 assorted Chick tracts. Pick your favorites, order a supply and get started.
It's that simple!
Order online at www.chick.com.
Or call 909.987.0771

HELP NEW CONVERTS GROW SPIRITUALLY

In this book for Christians, Jack Chick uses cartoons to illustrate basic Bible concepts for Christians. A great gift for anyone who wants to grow spiritually.

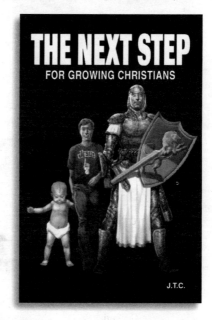

Covered topics include:

- How to pick a Bible
- Bible reading plan
- Why, how and what to pray
- A new way to love

- Defeating your enemy: Satan
- Traps to avoid
- The power of your testimony
- How to guide a sinner to Christ
- Your future rewards

#156 • 64 pages • paperback
Also in Spanish, German and Portuguese

OTHER BOOKS BY DAVID W. DANIELS

This book makes it easy to see how a Babylon goddess became the Virgin Mary. Well-researched, it pulls together centuries of history to show how Satan's ancient religion of Babylon still lives today as modern Roman Catholicism.

224 pages, paperback

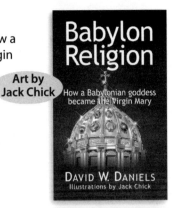

This easy-reading book, with cartoons by Jack Chick, shows the two histories of the Bible. One is of God preserving His words through His people. The other is of the devil using Roman Catholic "scholars" to pervert God's words. Learn how we got modern Bibles and why they are dangerous counterfeits.

160 pages, paperback

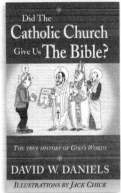

Here, respected linguist David W. Daniels answers many difficult questions people throw at the King James. If you want to defend the KJV or learn which Bible you can trust, the answers are here.

221 pages, paperback

Order at: **www.chick.com**
Or call: **909.987.0771**